Mabel H. Burgevin

Gift of Frederick

THE WHITE STEED

AND

COGGERERS

THE WHITE STEED

AND

COGGERERS

BY

PAUL VINCENT CARROLL

RANDOM HOUSE · NEW YORK

COPYRIGHT, 1939, BY

RANDOM HOUSE, INC.

———

Printed in the United States of America

———

*All rights reserved. No part of this book
may be reproduced in any form without
the permission of Random House, Inc.*

CAUTION: Professionals and amateurs are hereby warned
that *The White Steed* and *Coggerers,* being fully protected under the copyright laws of the United States of
America, the British Empire, including the Dominion of
Canada, and all other countries of the copyright union, are
subject to royalties. All rights, including professional,
amateur, motion picture, recitation, public reading, radio
broadcasting, and the rights of translation into foreign lan-
guages are strictly reserved. In their present form these
plays are dedicated to the reading public only. All in-
quiries regarding these plays should be addressed to
Richard J. Madden Play Company, at the Paramount
Building, Broadway and 43rd Street, New York City, N. Y.

FIRST PRINTING

*Frontispiece photograph of Paul Vincent Carroll by
Carl Van Vechten*

MANUFACTURED IN THE UNITED STATES OF AMERICA

To

Geоrge Jean Nathan
IN APPRECIATION OF HIS HAVING HELPED
A CERTAIN LAME DOG OVER A STILE

THE WHITE STEED

"You are still wrecked among heathen dreams . . ."
W. B. YEATS

AUTHOR'S NOTE

This play is symbolically based on the old pre-Christian tale of Ossian, the son of Finn, who was taken away by the lovely Niam on her white steed to the Land of Youth. Returning 300 years later in search of Finn, he finds all the great heroes dead and the land swarming with priests and little black men. One day he contemptuously leans down from the white steed and hurls into the air a flag of marble that one hundred of the little men are vainly trying to raise, but in doing so, he breaks the saddle girth and as his feet touch the earth, he withers miserably away. . . .

THE WHITE STEED was produced by Eddie Dowling at the Cort Theatre on January 10, 1939, with the following cast:

(*In order of appearance*)

CANON MATT LAVELLE	*Barry Fitzgerald*
ROSIEANNE (his housekeeper)	*Leslie Bingham*
FATHER SHAUGHNESSY	*George Coulouris*
PHELIM FINTRY	*Ralph Cullinan*
NORA FINTRY (his daughter)	*Jessica Tandy*
DONNACHAIDH MCGIOLLA PHADRAIG (the local district justice)	*Roland Bottomley*
PATRICK HEARTY	*Farrell Pelly*
SARAH HEARTY (his wife)	*Grace Mills*
BRIGID BRODIGAN	*Elizabeth Malone*
DENIS DILLON	*Liam Redmond*
INSPECTOR TOOMEY (head of the local police)	*Thomas P. Dillon*
MEG MAGEE (Father Shaughnessy's servant)	*Florence Barrett*
MICHAEL SHIVERS	*Tom Tully*

Staged by HUGH HUNT
Settings by WATSON BARRATT

SCENES

ACT ONE

The living room of Canon Matt Lavelle's Parochial House in the seaside village of Lorcan, County Louth, Ireland.

ACT TWO

Phelim Fintry's cottage—the following evening.

ACT THREE

Scene I. Canon Matt Lavelle's Parochial House. One week later.

Scene II. The same. That evening.

The time is the present.

ACT ONE

SCENE: *A sitting room in the local Parochial House in Lorcan, a small seaside place overlooking Carlingford Bay, and overlooked in turn by the Southern Range of the Mourne Hills. The furniture and fittings of the room are commonplace and typical. A sideboard, a bookcase, a few heavy tables and an occasional table, a miniature altar of the Blessed Virgin with a light; on the walls a selection of those sanguinary holy picture oleographs that make the atmosphere of the average Catholic house so oppressive. An old radio set with a battery. A window, back center, giving a glimpse of a hedge and gardens and a church wall. A door, left, to the kitchen, a door, back right, to the corridor at the front entrance. At the fireplace, right, is a large heavy armchair in which the parish priest,* CANON MATT LAVELLE, *sits. He looks frail and worn except in the eyes which gleam with feeling and occasionally with humor. He has had a shock which has paralyzed his legs which rest on a cushioned footrest near the chair. A large rug is wrapped about his body; his glasses hang from his neck by a black cord, a pillow supports his head which has fallen to the side in repose. He has dropped asleep. The minutes pass, he suddenly wakens with a start and looks about him anxiously. He becomes quite panicky.*

It is the afternoon of an autumn day in our own time.

CANON

God bless my soul! (*Looking about him, panicky*) Rosie-

3

anne! Rosieanne! (*Pause*) Och, where's the woman got to?
(ROSIEANNE, *an elderly housekeeper, enters.*)

ROSIEANNE
(*A little testily*)
Oh, are you wakened again, Canon?

CANON
Am I wakened again? 'Tis the cute oul' woman's way you
have of gettin' me to doze over. I'm a contrary oul' divil, I
suppose.

ROSIEANNE
If I'm always to be running in and out to you how am I to
be gettin' the ironin' and the washin' done and Father Shaughnessy's dinner and the . . .

CANON
And the clatterin' you do have with the postman and the
milkman, and the coal man and the cabbage man. It would
never do to miss *them*.

ROSIEANNE
Och, Canon, you're not behind at havin' a wee clatter yourself. And I'm leavin' next week anyway, so you'll soon be rid
of me.

CANON
(*Disturbed*)
You're what? There! I knew what this clatterin' of yours
would lead to. You're going to marry the coal man.

ROSIEANNE
I am not.

CANON
Well, it's the bread man.

4

ROSIEANNE

No, no, nor the postman either, even if he did ask me. I'm leavin' because no one but a saint could stick that new Father Shaughnessy that's here in your place.

CANON

I—well now, Rosieanne, I'll—I'll speak to him about you.

ROSIEANNE

Much good that would do. The only one he listens to is himself.

CANON

(*Making a brave show*)

Wait now, and I'll put—put down me foot.

ROSIEANNE

Faith, what foot have you to put down, God help you. And even if you had, isn't he never done warning the people from the altar that the Bishop gave him full charge while you're laid up.

CANON

But, good Lord, woman, even if I am crippled with the same damn paralysis, am I not the Canon still?

ROSIEANNE

Maybe so, but you are a big gun no longer, Canon.

CANON

(*Angrily*)

You wicked oul' spawn to say that to me! And I as fit as a fiddle if you'd count me legs out. (*Pause. He looks at her*) Listen to me, Rosieanne, where is he now?

5

ROSIEANNE

He's down in the church hall havin' a meetin'. Sure he's always havin' meetin's inside and outside and everywhere.

CANON

The divil of such a man for meetin's I ever met.

ROSIEANNE

If you had to hear him last night below at the pier, standin' on the promenade wall. Down with the drink, down with the dancin', down with the lovemakin', a solid Catholic nation for a holy Catholic people, and a dig at the wee handful of Protestants in every line. (*A knock without.*)

CANON

Who will that be, Rosieanne? If it's Father Shaughnessy wheel me out of here into me bedroom. He'll only start on me with these new schemes of his and aggravate me.

ROSIEANNE
(*Looking from the window*)
It's only Phelim Fintry that has the vegetable nursery.

CANON
(*As she is going*)
Here now, before you go out there for a clatter with Phelim, turn me on the wireless till I hear yon Father O'Dooley's football summary from Athlone.

ROSIEANNE

It's not his time yet, but there! (*As she switches on*) Will that satisfy you? (*She goes. Buzzing sound and a few plops from the radio, then the voice of the* ANNOUNCER *is heard.*)

ANNOUNCER

In the British House of Commons today, the Secretary of the Dominions replying to a question put by Major Walter Sorefoot as to whether it was really a fact that Great Britain had frittered away her honor, her safety and her sanity by handing over the Treaty Ports to the Southern Ireland Government, said that the answer to the first part of the gallant Major's question was no, and to the second part yes. A supplementary question by Mr. Stanislaska as to whether the proper name of Southern Ireland was not now Eire was drowned in cries of Order! Order! from the Government benches. (ROSIEANNE *re-enters, carrying a letter.*)

CANON

(*Irascibly*)

Father O'Dooley's not on yet. Turn off that nonsense, Rosieanne, themselves and their news. You'd think, be heavens, that the *Independent* was done away with. (*She turns off the radio*) By the way, where *is* me *Independent?* Now, did you . . .

ROSIEANNE

You're sittin' on it.

CANON

(*Mollified*)

So I am. (*He places it on his knee*) And you needn't snap the nose off me.

ROSIEANNE

Here's a note for you from Phelim Fintry, the vegetable man, and he has a nose on him like an iceberg.

7

CANON

(*Handling the note*)

Phelim with a nose on him to *me!* You're dotin', woman. It's his dues that he forgot to pay last month. Here, see what it says. Sure I can't see B from a bull's foot since I got the stroke.

ROSIEANNE

(*Tearing and opening it*)

It's a bill.

CANON

A what?

ROSIEANNE

An account.

CANON

You're blatherin'; you have it upside down.

ROSIEANNE

It's a bill, I'm tellin' you, for vegetables. Canon Matt Lavelle to Phelim Fintry, Debtor. To amount of account for vegetables from April, 1925, to December, 1937—£17.4.6d. Now has he a nose on him?

CANON

Show it here to me. (*He takes and peers at the paper*) So it is. Did he not tell me fifty times that I'd get me vegetables free till the two of us were under the clay? He's lost the grace of God, that's what it is. (*Pause*) What do *you* know about this?

ROSIEANNE

Well, I didn't want to annoy you, Canon, but it's about Phelim's daughter, Nora, that's in the lendin' library. The

8

girl that was away in England. Father Shaughnessy put her out of the hockey team yesterday.

CANON

And what's he got agin *her?* Sure, Nora's a fine little bit of a girl.

ROSIEANNE

It was for going with—with a boy.

CANON

(*Impatiently*)

A boy! And what the hell does he want her to go with, an elephant?

ROSIEANNE

He has the girls in the team pledged agin boys an' coortin' an' kissin'.

CANON

And the marriage rate the lowest in Europe. And he had to pick on Phelim's daughter. There's me leeks and scullions and carrots and a grand wallop of cauliflower every week, all gone in the one sweep.

ROSIEANNE

That's little of it. Wait till this new Vigilance Committee of his gets to work.

CANON

What *is* this affair that I hear all the blatherin' about?

ROSIEANNE

It's men and women he is havin' roamin' about the place seein' there is no kissin' on the roads, or bad dancin' or mixin' with Protestants and that District Justice with the new Irish name—he used to be Danny Fitzpatrick—promises that all

9

people brought before him by the Vigilance Committee will be severely dealt with.

CANON

Och, that oul' Bury-me-Grannie was in the Junior School in Maynooth when I was ordained. I think they put him out because he wouldn't wash his ears. (FATHER SHAUGHNESSY *enters, carrying a pile of papers and a load of books which he places on the tables irascibly. He is a tall, thin figure, with dark features, circumspect and mathematically-minded. There is under his equanimity the hint of cruelty. He is in the early thirties.*)

FATHER SHAUGHNESSY

Mud! Mud! Everywhere I go.

CANON

Where did you get *them?*

FATHER SHAUGHNESSY

I confiscated them from your free lending library down the street, Canon. I want to have a talk with you, a serious talk.

CANON
(*Wriggling uncomfortably*)
I'm none too well today.

FATHER SHAUGHNESSY
(*Spreading out papers on the table and preparing to work*)
About this campaign of mine, Canon, which I hope will spread throughout the nation—

ROSIEANNE

Father Shaughnessy, Canon Matt's not well enough to be discussin' and talkin'. The doctor said it.

FATHER SHAUGHNESSY
(*Curtly*)
Go to the kitchen, Rose, and stay there until you are wanted.

ROSIEANNE
As you say, Father. (*To the* CANON) Canon, I'm givin' you a month's notice as from today.

CANON
(*Crying out*)
Now you can't do that on me, Rosieanne.

FATHER SHAUGHNESSY
Your notice is accepted. Now go. (ROSIEANNE *goes very quietly, but very hurt.* CANON *peers after her forebodingly*) That woman's a bit too forward, Canon. I'd like my own servant from Derry City here, if it could be managed.

CANON
I'm afraid I—I couldn't get along without Rosieanne.

FATHER SHAUGHNESSY
And I can't get on *with* her.

CANON
(*Fearfully*)
Then it looks as if we'll have to have the two of them.

FATHER SHAUGHNESSY
(*Grimly*)
We'll leave it just now. There are more important matters I want to take up with you. First there is these books which I found in the library.

CANON

If you took all them, there mustn't be many left.

FATHER SHAUGHNESSY

There is sufficient. (*Pause*) Here the laxity is incredible. Dean Swift's filth, Bernard Shaw's blasphemous humor, AE's pantheistic cant, and the ravings of a humbug called Henrik Ibsen, and a score of others here all either blasphemous or anti-Catholic, or both. I may say that I received nothing but unwarranted liberties and impertinence from that girl assistant whose appointment *you* sanctioned in the library, so with the help of Mr. McGiolla Phadraig, the District Justice, I had her summarily censured and suspended.

CANON

In the name of God, do you mean the girl Nora Fintry?

FATHER SHAUGHNESSY

I believe that is her name.

CANON

But you put her out of the hockey team, too.

FATHER SHAUGHNESSY

Well, rules must be kept and spiritual laws respected. (*Pause*) Do you realize, Canon, just how bad a way this parish is in?

CANON
(*Lamely*)

Well, the people's poor and we can't take blood out of a stone.

FATHER SHAUGHNESSY

I mean neither blood nor stones. I mean moral laxity, spiritual carelessness and a general hardening of moral feelings.

12

(*He taps the table with his pencil*) I don't like it, Canon, and there's no use in mincing words.

CANON

There may be a little waywardness here and there, but bless me soul, the people's all right deep down.

FATHER SHAUGHNESSY

Not a bit. That old pretension won't do any longer. We have new enemies now to contend with like Communism, open godlessness and militant Atheism. And that's not mentioning four forced marriages here since I came two months ago.

CANON

There has always been a percentage of human weakness in every community since David dragged Bethsabee out of her bath.

FATHER SHAUGHNESSY

That is not an apologia I can accept. I mean to work in close conjunction with the Civil Law and I intend to make full use of the new law in the Constitution against public impropriety. I have already publicly announced that I will not, under any circumstances, baptize any illegitimate child or any child of a mixed marriage.

CANON

That's just being high-handed. You can't make Catholicism a mere code of morals wrapped up in the fear of God.

FATHER SHAUGHNESSY

Even if it were only a code of morals, that would be preferable to a sentimental puddle. I tell you, Canon, I have been all over England and I know what I'm talking about. There we have emotionalism in its worst forms, ruling head, heart and soul. No one there now thinks except in terms of how they feel at the moment, and they don't avoid evil because they love or fear God—they avoid it for ethical reasons. That is the reason why England has a percentage of goodness left, why her conduct is at times more reasonable than our own, but these methods are not good enough for us.

CANON
(*Mystified*)

It all seems very mystifying to me—maybe there's somethin' wrong with me and I still believe in poor human nature and the oul' grace of God.

FATHER SHAUGHNESSY

I'm afraid, Canon, there is a good slice of the clerical ostrich in you.

CANON
(*A little heated*)

I am no ostrich, nor a ferret either, but I *am* an oul' Irish sheepdog. I may be blind in the one eye and my fur is a bit tore with the furze and whins, but I know the dark well enough to round up me sheep and take them home.

FATHER SHAUGHNESSY
(*Quietly*)

I think I am annoying you, Canon, and you are not well.

CANON

Not a bit, I'm in good fightin' fettle the night.

FATHER SHAUGHNESSY

I will get Rose to bring you a glass of hot milk.

14

CANON

(*Crustily*)

You will not. The doctor stopped my wee thimbleful of spirits since I got the stroke and if I can't have that I'm certainly not going to have hot milk. That's an old grannie's drink.

FATHER SHAUGHNESSY

Very well, then. (*Pause*) Do you happen to know the man Michael Shivers?

CANON

Sure, everyone knows Mick. It's he that has the Stella Maris Hotel below at the pier.

FATHER SHAUGHNESSY

He misses Mass quite frequently.

CANON

Maybe so, but sure the man put that roof up there over your head.

FATHER SHAUGHNESSY

You mean *your* head, Canon.

CANON

Well, *my* head then.

FATHER SHAUGHNESSY

And does that excuse him from missing Mass? Is that to serve as a permanent dispensation?

CANON

Often in these cases, time and the risin' grace of God fix things back the way they were without our blunderin' fingers. Mick will be all right in God's good time.

15

FATHER SHAUGHNESSY

That's just theological procrastination.

CANON

(*Irascibly*)

Ach, you're afflicted with a mathematical mind. You did teach mathematics in some college in England, didn't you, or was it in Derry?

FATHER SHAUGHNESSY

You say that to me because I feel conscientiously there are many abuses in this parish that should be stamped out.

CANON

I say it to you because you are looking for mathematical exactitudes in the spiritual and you'll not get them here so long as the Irish mind re-echoes back to the oak tree and the wishing well. In this country of ours, with all respect to your psychology and ethics, in spite of Governments and laws, the people here are fundamentally free. What you want is to replace their old wayward love of God that is splattered with mud and blood and crudities, with a shrinking fear of God that'll knock all the life out of them. If you want that sort of thing, go and live in Scotland, where the people have measured every word in the Bible with a screw gauge and knocked every ounce of beauty out of their national life, and what have they achieved? Merely a reputation for the Bible amongst intelligent people as the most volatile and dangerous book ever written.

FATHER SHAUGHNESSY

I am not here, Canon, to discuss an apostate nation. But I *am* here to learn whether you are with me or *against* me.

16

CANON

I don't see the need for this reforming craze of yours.

FATHER SHAUGHNESSY

You can say that after four girls last month having to be forcibly married and three or four mixed marriages and even the very schoolmaster courting a Protestant girl. I shall dismiss that man for this giving of scandal, if necessary.

CANON

(*Heatedly*)

You can't do that.

FATHER SHAUGHNESSY

And why not, Canon?

CANON

Sure, the man has such a whining fear of his bread and butter that he collects the money at the chapel door for us, he comes round with me when I am collecting my dues, he plays the organ in the chapel, he brings the loads of coppers to the bank for us. Sure, we'd be lost to the world without him.

FATHER SHAUGHNESSY

There's nothing extraordinary in these activities in a teacher. His successor can be made to do the same.

CANON

I am not so sure. Times are changing and the teachers now are getting nearly as important as the bank clerks. I admit that as a man he's a spittoon, but as a teacher he's a gem.

FATHER SHAUGHNESSY

He will be a brighter gem when I have settled with him. I have sent for him.

CANON

Do you mean him to come here?

FATHER SHAUGHNESSY

And what else? This house should be the hub and center here of moral activity.

CANON

You will be havin' him there cringin' and cryin' and I not well?

FATHER SHAUGHNESSY

I can't help that, Canon. I have also arranged for my new Vigilance Committee to meet me here at seven o'clock with their weekly report. If you like I will have you wheeled into the bedroom.

CANON

I can't afford a fire in the bedroom along with a fire here and a fire in the kitchen and I am not goin' to sit in the cold for any Vigilance Committee.

FATHER SHAUGHNESSY

Then, Canon, why not accept the Bishop's offer of refuge and quiet in the Aged Priests' Home outside of Dublin?

CANON

(Angrily)

I will accept no such offer and I am no aged priest. I am only sixty-seven and I am as fit as a fiddle if I could only walk. (Enter ROSIEANNE.)

ROSIEANNE

(To the CANON)

If you please, Canon Matt, Phelim Fintry wants a word with you.

18

CANON

Phelim again? Sure, show him in, Rosieanne. If *you* don't mind, Father.

FATHER SHAUGHNESSY

Not in the least. (ROSIEANNE *goes off*) I want to meet everyone here on a friendly footing.

CANON

Ach, sure, poor Phelim!

FATHER SHAUGHNESSY

Is this that girl Nora Fintry's father?

CANON

It is, and the only child he has. She was in England in some public library. She came home to get this job in the library here. Her mother died with the second child and Phelim never took another one.

FATHER SHAUGHNESSY

I had to suspend her for impertinent comments in the library and I found her a bad influence in the hockey team. England didn't do *her* any good.

CANON

It's grand to have England to blame everything on. If there had never been an England, the moralists of this country would have invented her. (ROSIEANNE *re-enters followed by* PHELIM FINTRY, *a quiet peasant of middle age.*)

ROSIE

Here's Phelim, Canon.

CANON

Sure, take a seat beside me here, Phelim, till I be havin' a crack with you.

PHELIM

(*Slowly taking a seat and looking at the* CANON)
I'm sorry to see you there, Canon Matt.

CANON

Och, sure I'll soon be as fit as a fightin' cock. Have you met
Father Shaughnessy yet?

PHELIM
(*Glancing over*)
I met him once at the waterfront.

FATHER SHAUGHNESSY
How do you do, Phelim?

PHELIM

I came down, Canon Matt, to see about what was wrong
that my daughter Nora was put out of the hockey team and
put out of the library, too.

FATHER SHAUGHNESSY
(*Interposing*)
Nora was suspended for impertinence unbecoming to an
Irish girl, and she was put out of the team by me, Phelim, for
breaking one of the rules of membership.

PHELIM
May I ask, Father, what rule?

FATHER SHAUGHNESSY
The rule, my good man, that forbids any of the members of
the hockey team from keeping company with a man.

PHELIM

And is it become a crime, Father, for a growin' woman like Nora to want to keep company?

FATHER SHAUGHNESSY

No, Phelim, it's not a crime, but the by-roads and the lanes and the dark places along the coast are not the proper places for furthering a Catholic courtship—such conduct must not be tolerated.

PHELIM

Can you tell me a better place then, Father Shaughnessy?

FATHER SHAUGHNESSY

As a good Catholic you should not need to be told that such a courtship should be conducted in your own house.

PHELIM

Do you know my house, Father Shaughnessy?

FATHER SHAUGHNESSY

I can't say I do, as yet.

PHELIM

(*Appealingly*)

It's a white-washed hovel with two rooms in it, built in 1829 with stone floors that killed me wife and the childer that were to be yet born to us. *I* sleep in the kitchen in a box bed and Nora sleeps in the wee room. It has a wooden bed and the bed-covers are not too new and the wee bits of furniture are wizened with the weather and there's a wee bit of curtain that Nora hangs her few Sunday belongings behind—a blue costume, a few pairs of stockings, and a cheap little dance frock. She might show you all these, Father, because as a min-

21

ister of God you might understand, but as a woman do you think she would like young fellows like Corr to see them?

FATHER SHAUGHNESSY

These things are of minor importance and I am concerned meantime with the graver issues. It is for you to say, Phelim Fintry, whether you're with me or against me in the cleaning up of our parish—in the words of our Lord "in the making straight of the crooked."

PHELIM

(*In a temper*)

All right, Father, you want to know what side I'm on. I'm on the side of me own blood.

CANON

Phelim, Phelim, I'm surprised at you. Sure, what talk is that?

FATHER SHAUGHNESSY

You have said sufficient to declare yourself, Phelim Fintry. You may go now.

PHELIM

I will go when I get what I came for.

FATHER SHAUGHNESSY

What did you come for if it wasn't just to make trouble?

PHELIM

I came for my daughter's good name, but seein' I can't get that I will take somethin' less. I will take the amount of my account for vegetables for fifteen years. It will help to make Nora's room more suitable for her friends. (*A knock.* NORA FINTRY *makes a defiant and dramatic entrance. She is a finely made girl in the twenties, quiet and pensive, but quick in*

22

spirit and temper. She regards them all frankly and without self-consciousness.)

NORA
(*Rather sharply*)

Father, what are you doing here?

PHELIM

I was talkin' to the Canon, sure.

NORA

Did you come here to beg for *me?*

PHELIM

I did not. You're puttin' a lie on me now.

NORA

I don't believe you. There's a bit of the oul' curryin' willie-wag-tail about you, but I will beg from no man and I will have no man beg *for* me either. Come along home out of this.

PHELIM

Sure, if you'd let me draw me breath—

CANON

You are in the divil's own temper, Nora, and you never even asked me how I was.

NORA
(*Not unkindly*)

You know I wish you well, Canon.

FATHER SHAUGHNESSY
(*Crossing to her*)

Nora Fintry, I am disappointed. I was expecting a more satisfactory visit from you.

23

NORA

You mean, Father Shaughnessy, you expected me to crawl to the porch of your parochial door and beg my job in the library back?

FATHER SHAUGHNESSY
(*With pain*)
I expected you to come here and correct your impertinent attitude to me, like any modest Irish maiden.

NORA

But I am not modest and some of your mob say I am not even a maiden, so I must live up to your opinion of me.

PHELIM
(*Interposing*)
Now there's no luck, Nora, in that sort of talk to the priest. Maybe I was a bit hasty meself with me tongue. If I was . . .

NORA

Aw, stop spilling your Irish dribbles, Father, and come home. (*She grasps him firmly by the arm and leads him out.* FATHER SHAUGHNESSY *stares fixedly after them.*)

CANON
(*Breaking out*)
Nora, I—I—I'm ashamed of you.

NORA
(*As she goes*)
Oh, no, you're not, Canon. Am *I* ashamed of *you* because you stumped when they wanted to send you to a home for clerical grannies?

CANON
(*As door closes*)
I—I—I, well, I— (*He subsides*) M—m, she's a corker, right enough!

FATHER SHAUGHNESSY
That girl has been ruined by what Britain very shrewdly calls broadmindedness.

CANON
Och, is it fair always to be throwing the British stone at her? These people will do anything for you if you rub them the right way.

FATHER SHAUGHNESSY
Catholicism is not a matter of rubbing people any way. I wish, Canon, you would accept the Bishop's offer and cease confusing me here.

CANON
(*Vehemently*)
Didn't I say my say about that? You may get rid of certain evils in this parish, Father Shaughnessy, but *I* won't be one of them. (*Calling in bad temper*) Rosieanne! Are you there, Rosieanne?

FATHER SHAUGHNESSY
(*Testily*)
Could we not have some sort of bell here instead of that bawling of yours? (ROSIEANNE *knocks and enters. She is perturbed.*)

ROSIEANNE
(*Painfully*)
Here's that new District Justice—Dan Fitzpatrick he used to be. I can't say his new name in Irish.

25

FATHER SHAUGHNESSY

You mean Donnachaidh McGiolla Phadraig. What does he want?

ROSIEANNE

You see, Father, he won't talk anything but Irish and I can't make him out.

FATHER SHAUGHNESSY

Stupid girl, go out and say "Tar isteac, agus failte romhat."

ROSIEANNE

Yes, Father. (*Opening the door and speaking*) "Tar isteac agus failte romhat." (*As the District Justice enters, she bows and goes. He is typical of the new Gaelic snob with all the vices of the British public school snob and few of his virtues. He is rotund, pompous, of the paterfamilias type.*)

FATHER SHAUGHNESSY

Ah, cionnus atha tu, a chara? Failte agus slainthe.

PHADRAIG

Dia dhuith, a athair, agus beannact Muire. Nac bhuil an Canon go maith fos?

FATHER SHAUGHNESSY

Ta a bhliadhna trom air. (*To the* CANON) Mr. McGiolla Phadraig is inquiring after you, Canon.

CANON

Is that what he's sayin'? Tell him from me "Suscipiat Dominus sacrificium de manibus tuis."

26

PHADRAIG

(*Laughing drily*)

Ha! Ha! The Canon is having his joke; I'm afraid I haven't the Latin, Canon.

CANON

Well, *I* haven't the Gaelic. Suppose we both lose our senses and talk in English. (*Dry laughter.*)

PHADRAIG

I only talk in the English when it simply can't be helped, Canon.

FATHER SHAUGHNESSY

A little English at the moment with the Canon and the Vigilance Committee would facilitate matters, Mr. McGiolla Phadraig.

PHADRAIG

If you desire it then, Father Shaughnessy, but I dislike these descents into the Saxon Beurla. Will His Reverence join us in the discussion?

FATHER SHAUGHNESSY

If you feel inclined, Canon . . .

CANON

What is the use? I won't agree with anything you say. I don't agree with this new tide of ideas. I am human enough to want, like all ordinary people, a little sugar in my tea, a little soda in my whiskey, a wee bit of coaxing in my dogma and a hot bottle in my bed on a frosty night. I hate anything in the raw from raw poteen to raw men like Calvin, whom I'd have strangled out of a sense of decency to the humanity Christ died for. If our Lord had never been human, had never drunk wine, had never allowed a woman's hair to clean

27

His feet, had never pitied a miserable little bitch selling herself in a narrow street, half the people who now believe in Him would have sput on Him long ago. No, I am not with you, I am agin you. You can laugh at me when I call my servant Rosieanne, instead of Rose, when I go mad for fresh vegetables and mashed potatoes, or when I read the *Independent;* but I believe, when I go down on my knees on the stone floor of that old Church out there, and ask God in my own way to forgive the human weaknesses of these poor slaves of ours, that I am doing more good than all the Calvinistic seekin'-out and spyin' and Vigilance Committees you propose. There now, I have said my say and in me heart I'm agin you.

FATHER SHAUGHNESSY

Canon, we must meet new dangers and new enemies with new weapons. That must be our apologia for our present activity.

PHADRAIG

An activity, Canon, that I consider imperative. In my District Court every week I am pained by the fact that the Court is not supposed to be a court of morals—a heretical legacy from British days.

FATHER SHAUGHNESSY

There is my point. Courts should be courts of morals as well as of laws and in this Catholic country it is time the Civil and the Ecclesiastical laws were one.

CANON

(*Bursting out*)

So that every time the State makes a blunder it can always blame the Church. It's a grand idea so far as the State is concerned. In a few generations from now every little snotherynosed philosopher will be denouncing the Church at the Market Squares for sending the lay martyrs of our time to jail and the boyos in the side streets will start collecting Spanish bullets. In my theory of things the weapon agin fear is prayer. Is Our Lady no longer invocable, and is the Sacred Heart become a design for the postage stamps of the New Eire? (*A knock without.* ROSIEANNE *enters.*)

ROSIEANNE

The members of Father Shaughnessy's Vigilance Committee is here, Canon. Will I let them in?

CANON

Phut! The Daniels come to judgment!

FATHER SHAUGHNESSY

Show them in, Rose. (*She goes*) Canon, if you are not with us, I hope you will not show yourself against us.

CANON

I'm neither with you nor agin you. There was never yet a law made that was stronger than the life Christ loved and pitied.

ROSIEANNE
(*Entering*)

This is them, Father. (*The Vigilance Committee enter. They consist of* PATRICK HEARTY, *a tall, rough-spoken man; his wife* SARAH HEARTY, *a stout, tempestuous moralist;* BRIGID BRODIGAN, *a thin, scraggy virgin of forty. They gaze about them looking solemn and stupid.*)

PHADRAIG

Dia dhibh.

29

ALL

Dia agus Muire.

SARAH

And the same to you, Canon, God help you.

CANON

Och, it's you, Sarah Hearty, is it? Tell me, did you stop that youngster of yours from filling dung for Andie Mac-Arthur and send him back to school as I told you?

FATHER SHAUGHNESSY

These things must wait just now, Canon. We have important matters before us.

CANON

Oh, don't let *me* keep you back. (*Pause*) Is that yourself I see there, Brigid Brodigan? I thought you told me a while ago you had Andie MacArthur and the farm by the tail.

BRIGID

Och, sure his daughter came home from America, Canon, and put the notion off him.

CANON

And is that why you're here?

BRIGID

Sure, I must be doin' somethin' useful, Canon.

FATHER SHAUGHNESSY

Canon, please!

CANON

Och, sure, isn't it so long since I've seen them. Sure, the day I got the stroke wasn't I below at the hedge with Patrick

Hearty helping him to tighten a bit of wire over the gap where his cow broke through and there he is sitting as if I was dead and a twenty pound headstone on top of me.

HEARTY
(*Spluttering*)

Sure—sure—Canon, I—I—

CANON

That's enough. You have your front pushed out now be-cause you're on the Vigilance Committee but was it two times or three I lifted you by the backside of the britches out of the drain and the drink on you? (*Furiously*) For two pins I'd rise and wool the oul' head off you.

FATHER SHAUGHNESSY
(*Shortly*)

Canon, my patience is about exhausted. These good people have pledged themselves to me to be an example to the others in this parish, and I have the greatest faith in them. Now will you please rest yourself and let us go ahead.

CANON

I will. I will rest myself. (*With a snort*) Hey, you there, Rosieanne. (*A knock.* ROSIEANNE *enters.*)

ROSIEANNE

Do you want me, Canon?

CANON

Do I want you, woman. Come and turn me round to the fire and fix this pillow under me head. (*She makes the* CANON *comfortable*) There now, I will maybe sleep and if I do, waken me at seven for me chicken broth and don't forget to put the grated carrot in it.

ROSIEANNE

I will, Canon. (*She crosses*) Is there anything else, Father Shaughnessy?

FATHER SHAUGHNESSY

If Mr. Dillon, the schoolmaster, calls, show him in here at once.

ROSIEANNE

Yes, Father. (*She goes.* CANON *sighs and settles into his pillows.*)

FATHER SHAUGHNESSY

My good people, we are met here this evening for important work, and I am glad to say that the District Justice, Mr. McGiolla Phadraig, is giving us his full co-operation. (*Murmurs of approval and a bow from* PHADRAIG) Now, my good people, I don't want you to get into your heads that our work here is to make us cruel or unjust or unkind. Far from it. Each of us must have in him the simple love of God and of all His creatures; that begins and ends everything. How could we dare to be cruel or unjust or unkind when we are pledged to do God's work and the work of His Holy Church? That would make God angry with us and who would want that saddest of misfortunes? But at the same time we must not confuse kindness with weakness. We must not think firmness and resolution in our duties unjust and we must not be led by lax people into believing that a holy sternness resembles cruelty.

ALL

Hear, hear! Father.

THE WHITE STEED

FATHER SHAUGHNESSY

Now, as I told you at our previous talks, there are evils about us we must grapple with and we must not shirk that duty merely because it is unpleasant. You will endorse that, Mr. McGiolla Phadraig.

PHADRAIG

Most heartily. Duty is often unpleasant, but it is none the less duty. For example, it pains me tonight as part of my duty to speak in the Saxon tongue.

HEARTY

As the temporary spokesman of this Committee meeting, I say we heartily endorse all that you and Mr. McGiolla Phadraig have said. As one connected for a lifetime with the old-womanish policy of the Young Men's Society, I can say this was all long overdue.

ALL

Hear, hear!

HEARTY

(*Encouraged*)

We must fearlessly unfurl the banner of the Cross, ladies and gentlemen . . . (*A long snore from the* CANON. *All turn and stare at the back of his head.* ROSIEANNE *knocks and enters.*)

ROSIEANNE

Mr. Dillon, the schoolmaster, Your Reverence. (DENIS DILLON, *a young man in the twenties, enters. He is ill at ease, awkward and a little breathless. He is obviously perturbed.* ROSIEANNE *bends over the* CANON, *and then goes.*)

DILLON

You—sent for me, Your Reverence. (*With a look at the* CANON) Or was it the Canon, maybe?

33

FATHER SHAUGHNESSY

It was I. (*Pointing to a chair*) Sit down, Mr. Dillon.

DILLON

(*Awkwardly*)

I—I hope there's nothing wrong, Father.

FATHER SHAUGHNESSY

Nothing that cannot be righted. Mr. Dillon, I intended asking you to be the secretary of my new Vigilance Committee here.

DILLON

Thank you, Your Reverence. I'm kept rather busy with other duties, but if you think . . .

FATHER SHAUGHNESSY

One moment. I find on reading the weekly report of the Committee that you see here before you, that not only are you ineligible for that honor but that you are, in addition, very much at variance with its aims and objects in your private life.

DILLON

(*Fearfully*)

If it's the drink you mean, Father, sure it's only occasionally that I . . .

FATHER SHAUGHNESSY

Drink! (*A pause. He consults report*) There's no mention of alcoholic excess here. In justice to you we shall consider your remark as not having been heard.

PHADRAIG

An able and excellent ruling, Father Shaughnessy.

THE WHITE STEED

FATHER SHAUGHNESSY

We must not forget we are doing God's work.

ALL

Hear, hear!

FATHER SHAUGHNESSY

Mr. Dillon. The report against you is concerned with your relations with a girl of alien faith. (*Pause*) You have the right to deny the allegation. What do you say?

DILLON

(*Tensely afraid*)

I admit I am keeping company with Dorothy Craig.

FATHER SHAUGHNESSY

And she's not a Catholic?

DILLON

(*Pathetically*)

She's a good girl.

PHADRAIG

(*Leaning forward*)

You must answer the Reverend President's question, Mr. Dillon.

DILLON

She's not a Catholic. (*Pause.*)

SARAH

Is it true you're daft in love with her?

FATHER SHAUGHNESSY

That is hardly a relevant question. A direction, Mr. Mc-Giolla Phadraig.

35

PHADRAIG

It may safely be ignored.

BRIGID

But it's true. I can prove it.

FATHER SHAUGHNESSY

There is no need to prove what is irrelevant.

BRIGID

What does irrelevant mean, Father? I had to leave school when I was ten. Can we not have ordinary talk?

FATHER SHAUGHNESSY

The matter is closed.

BRIGID

Closed or open, Your Reverence, there's plenty of good Catholic girls in Lorcan but I suppose they are not good enough for the schoolmaster.

SARAH

(*Irascibly*)

Och, it's yourself you mean, shut up!

BRIGID

I'm insulted! I'll walk out!

FATHER SHAUGHNESSY

(*Knocking on the table*)

I would remind everyone here that we are doing the work of God. Spite, envy and injurious words are not part of it.

PHADRAIG

Excellent. I advise all of you to take a lesson from the mildness and forbearance of His Reverence.

36

FATHER SHAUGHNESSY

You see, Mr. Dillon, we do not want to be hard on you.

DILLON

(*Tensely thankful*)

I know I am entirely in your hands.

FATHER SHAUGHNESSY

If you are, you are in good hands. Now, Mr. Dillon, this grave admission of yours that you keep company with a girl of alien faith is regrettable. Need I say, Mr. Dillon, that as a responsible resident here and that as a faithful servant of the Holy Church, your duty is clear?

DILLON

Do you mean that—I'm to give her up?

SARAH

He's engaged to her, Father. I happen to know, but it's a secret.

BRIGID

An' he's afraid of a breach of promise agin him. (DILLON *hangs his head.*)

PHADRAIG

An anomaly, Father, that will be swept away when the Civil and the Ecclesiastical laws are united in this Catholic country. In my opinion, for a Court to award breach damages against a Catholic to a girl of another faith is contrary to Catholic morality.

FATHER SHAUGHNESSY

I was just going to remark on that. It seems almost incredible that in this country civil and religious writs should be

37

at variance. (*Pause*) Nevertheless, Mr. Dillon must have moral courage. Come, Mr. Dillon, I am sure you have your answer ready for us.

DILLON

It's hard, Father. These things are always hard.

PHADRAIG

That is not an answer in law, my good sir.

DILLON

She'd maybe turn—Catholic for me.

SARAH

The Craigs to turn Catholic! A crowd of black Billy Boys from Belfast!

PHADRAIG

Have you any evidence, Mr. Dillon, to support the supposition that this girl would turn Catholic for you?

DILLON

She—she sometimes comes in with me and sits in the Chapel when I'm at confession.

PHADRAIG

That is a mere act of courtesy in which these Protestants excel, but it is not evidence.

FATHER SHAUGHNESSY

If this girl turns Catholic it is one more in the true fold and is a good and proper action in the sight of God. Let us not be hard on Mr. Dillon. Let us allow him to sit yonder for a while and make up his mind. (*He points to a chair apart.*)

HEARTY

What while does he need, to choose between the right and the wrong, Father?

FATHER SHAUGHNESSY

That is so, Mr. Hearty, but we dare not be otherwise than sympathetic and forbearing.

DILLON
(Dejectedly)

Thank you for that at least, Father. (*He rises and crosses slowly to the chair*) If—if I'm not able, what is to be done?

PHADRAIG
(Gravely)

We must all subordinate ourselves to the common good, Mr. Dillon.

DILLON
(Sitting dejectedly)

I wish I could be strong either way. I—I'm like something dangling between earth and water.

FATHER SHAUGHNESSY
(Evenly)

If you feel, Mr. Dillon, you are too weak-willed to pass the test of moral and spiritual sobriety, you can, of course, hand me in your resignation from the school.

DILLON
(Rising dumbfounded)

My—my resignation. You can't mean that, Father?

39

FATHER SHAUGHNESSY
(With a hint of cruelty)

I am very patient, but I never trifle with words. *(Pause)* Pray collect your thoughts, Mr. Dillon, if you must have thought between right and wrong.

DILLON
(Dejectedly sitting down again)

I—I will— *(He sits, his head dropped on his hands. He peers out into space, and takes no notice of the others, who go on with their work at the table.)*

FATHER SHAUGHNESSY
(Resuming)

Let us proceed. *(Pause)* You have just seen a man being put severely to the test. *(Pause)* God forbid that any of us here should feel harshly about him, should feel other than sympathetic, but this sympathy must not extend to weakness. It must not give you false shame or false sentiment.

PHADRAIG

Let me tell you, my friends, as a judge, that false emotion is ever and always dangerous in cases where it can be confused with pity.

FATHER SHAUGHNESSY

Mr. McGiolla Phadraig has given you a very wise direction. Is there any further business to report, Patrick Hearty?

HEARTY
(Shuffling papers)

There is a letter here, Father, signed by the people that own the four hotels at the waterfront. They complain that our request to Mr. McGiolla Phadraig to refuse licenses to

dance halls unless the programme is exclusively Irish is going
to chase the holiday visitors away.

FATHER SHAUGHNESSY

Have you any comment to make on this, Mr. McGiolla
Phadraig?

PHADRAIG

(*Smugly*)

None, except that I shall continue to refuse such applica-
tions in my official capacity.

SARAH

Sure, the four hussies that had to get married last month
were never out of these dance halls.

FATHER SHAUGHNESSY

I have already noted that fact. You will inform these people,
Patrick Hearty, that the Vigilance Committee will take no
action. Is there any further business?

HEARTY

There's a letter here, Father, from Dermot Corr, the boy
that caused the trouble in the hockey team with Nora Fintry.

FATHER SHAUGHNESSY

He should come here instead of writing. What has he to
say for himself?

HEARTY

He says he's ready to come and make a full explanation—
that there was nothin' between him and Nora Fintry, and
that if she's agin the priest he wants to have nothin' at all to
do with her.

BRIGID

Didn't he stand up for the girl at the row and defy the priest?

HEARTY

He says he's sorry for that—that it was in the heat of the moment.

PHADRAIG

I think that is a very frank and courageous statement from this young man.

FATHER SHAUGHNESSY

And so do I. It has courage and clear-sightedness.

HEARTY

Will I send him a pardon, Father?

FATHER SHAUGHNESSY

You may. A fiery youngster, but a good boy for all that. He'd make an excellent collector for the chapel. Make a note of him, Patrick Hearty, in case Mr. Dillon doesn't win his battle over there. (*All turn and look at* DILLON.)

HEARTY

I will, Father.

FATHER SHAUGHNESSY

Does that conclude the business for today?

BRIGID

There's the matter of the Fintry girl, Father.

SARAH

Better tell His Reverence, Patrick, what Neil O'Donovan that's home from England told you about her.

HEARTY

Neil O'Donovan, home on holiday, Father, says she was a bit of a—a wanton on the other side.

PHADRAIG

Does he mention a specific instance of misconduct?

HEARTY

Not actually, sir, but you know how it is with a fellow who can't say too much.

FATHER SHAUGHNESSY

I don't think we should proceed on hearsay. We should judge this girl according to her attitude here amongst us, put aside spite and prejudice and leave every avenue open to her to come here submissively as Dermot Corr did and be one of us.

BRIGID

The hussy is too deep in her for that, Father.

FATHER SHAUGHNESSY

We will consider that remark of yours, Brigid Brodigan, as not heard.

PHADRAIG

Excellent. An open mind, my good woman, is the floor of justice.

FATHER SHAUGHNESSY

I will see the girl myself at her house. (*He rises and all rise after him*) That, I think, will be all for the moment. Go out now, to your ordinary work in your ordinary way, but keep your eyes open and your ears, but at the same time, your hearts. (*He hands them all cards*) These cards, bearing my signature, and that of Mr. McGiolla Phadraig will admit you to the dance halls and to the public houses and invest you with special powers, as my moral policemen. You will each make a detailed report at our next meeting. (*Pause*) And now, Mr. Dillon! (*All turn and look at* DILLON. *He raises his head slowly. He rises weakly from the chair and comes forward, a meek man. A long pause.*)

DILLON

I—I will do what you want. I will not see Dorothy Craig again.

FATHER SHAUGHNESSY

Excellent. Your victory is an example to the rest. Give me your hand, Mr. Dillon. (DILLON *gives him his hand weakly.* FATHER SHAUGHNESSY *shakes it*) I congratulate you and, as a reward for your courage, I appoint you secretary of this Vigilance Committee. (DILLON *nods abjectly.*)

DILLON

I will do what I am capable of doing. Thank you. I don't feel well. I'll go now if I may. (*He turns and goes quietly. The rest follow him out except* FATHER SHAUGHNESSY *and* MR. MC GIOLLA PHADRAIG.)

PHADRAIG

Well, Father Shaughnessy, I think we have reason to congratulate ourselves. The work is begun and we are on the way to a purely Catholic State.

FATHER SHAUGHNESSY

True, but the battle that is to re-echo outside this parish has yet to be fought. (*They go out quietly together. The minutes pass. The* CANON *starts and mutters in his sleep, then he sits up, rubs his head and looks sleepily at the empty chairs. He sniffs and calls fussily.)*

CANON
(Calling)
Rosieanne, Rosieanne! (ROSIEANNE *enters.*)

ROSIEANNE
Oh, you're wakened again, Canon, are you? Do you want me?

CANON
(Sleepily pointing to the window)
Oscal an—an—an fhuinneog.

Curtain

ACT TWO

ACT TWO

SCENE: PHELIM FINTRY's *Cottage. The following evening.*
A shabby living room, with soiled whitewashed walls, and wizened odds and ends of furniture; some chairs round an open grate with hobs. A door, left, to the road. A door, right, to NORA's *bedroom. A screened-off bed in the corner, left back.*

PHELIM FINTRY *is discovered seated on a low stool, in his shirt sleeves, by the fireside, reading a paper through old spectacles.* NORA FINTRY *is making griddle cakes at a deal table, center. She is pensively reciting aloud, as she works, a verse of Longfellow's poem. . . .*

NORA
I remember the black wharves and the slips,
And the sea-tides tossing free,
And Spanish sailors with bearded lips
And the beauty and mystery of the ships,
And the magic of the sea. . . .

(*After a moment,* PHELIM *puts down the paper silently, and regards her. There is a pause.*)

PHELIM
Did you hear, Nora, that Dermot Corr was before the new priest's Committee?

NORA
(*Coming out of reverie*)
I did. How could Committees live if there were no Dermot Corrs . . . ?

49

PHELIM

They will be expectin' you to go too, Nora. If you refuse, you will have the priest agin you.

NORA

So long as God is not agin me. . . .

PHELIM

It's not what God says here. It's what the priest says, and you must live. Over where you were in England, a girl was a human craythur like a man, but here she's either a servant girl or a mortal sin.

NORA

Maybe so, but I'm going to try being a woman instead.

PHELIM

If that means fightin' the priest, I'd rather you'd go back to England.

NORA

I'm not going. I belong here, and here I stay. I'm going to work for Michael Shivers, that owns the Stella Maris Hotel at the waterfront. He wants a girl that can receive Cross Channel visitors and look after the accounts.

PHELIM

(*Surprised*)

And you never told me! That'll be in place of his wife that ran away with that American tourist that used to be always looking for the melons and the peanuts. They say himself and the new priest don't get on.

NORA

That's all to the good if there's going to be a fight.

PHELIM

You poor innocent! You'll fight alone. So long as they have the altar, they have the whip with the long lash on it. Didn't you see for yourself how thev made Dillon, the school-master, creep?

NORA

Poor devil. Brave only when he gets the drink he sneaks out of the Stella Maris, and he gets the shakers when he sees a Roman collar in a shop window. (*A knock without.*)

PHELIM

If this is any of them, let you mind your foolish tongue. Come in! (DENIS DILLON *enters. He is maudlin with drink.*)

DILLON

Can I come in for a minute?

NORA

(*Belligerently*)

You may, if you bow three times to the cat and beg the dog's pardon.

PHELIM

Come on in, Denis, an' don't mind her.

DILLON

(*Coming forward*)

The worst of it is, I can't answer her. Nora, as a good Christian, I admire you and hate the sight of you, because you are not afraid of your masters. There now, in vino veritas.

PHELIM

You have been havin' a half one, Denis. Sit down and rest yourself.

DILLON

(*Sitting*)

Yes, Phelim, I have been having a half one. I have been having ten half ones. Half ones make me brave. Half ones change me from a man who loves law and hates life to a man who loves life and to blazes with law. Half ones take away my fear of my holy masters, my fear of my job and the road. That's it, the road. To you, Nora, the road is a place winding out and upwards to the stars; to me it is a lane down to an old pond where men drown themselves because they have nothing to eat.

PHELIM

Get him a drop of tea, Nora, for to clear his head.

NORA

(*Looking at him*)

I suppose as a woman I should be sorry for you, but I'm not. I despise you.

PHELIM

Can't you leave him alone!

DILLON

No, let her go on. I know she hates me. Hate and love and fear, the real trinity under the statues and the prayers and the hymns. I'm sayin' it. I'm tellin' you, mind, and I wouldn't say it only for the whiskey in me makin' me brave.

NORA

It's a poor kind of bravery that whiskey gives. Have you nothing better than that to bring out the good in you?

PHELIM

Nice good it's bringing out in him . . . blasphemy an' blatherin'.

52

NORA

(*Giving him a cup of tea*)

Here, drink this. For two pins I'd throw the damned thing about you.

PHELIM

Nora!

DILLON

Do! I implore you, do. Throw it about me. I crave you to throw it about me.

NORA

That's right. Self-abasement and belly-crawling.

DILLON

I know. That and worse . . . the badge of all our tribe. Spit on me, throw mud on me, so that one day I may maybe find the extreme and by the living Christ I can turn and wreck red ruin, that's it! That's what's in me and I'd never have known it only the whiskey told me.

PHELIM

(*To* NORA)

That's enough. You'll only aggravate him and the drop in him. (*He claps* DILLON *on the back*) No one will give you your breakfast for that kind of high talk, Denis. You be a good sensible lad and mind your school.

DILLON

(*Coming out of reverie*)

School! (*Melancholy*) "The very name is like a bell to toll me back . . ." Och, I'm a fool, a poor idiot, a little black man. The whiskey's dyin' in me.

NORA

(*Humoring him*)

I didn't know you were a poet?

PHELIM

There you are, startin' him again.

DILLON

(*Morbidly*)

Nevertheless, Nora, I am a poet. I am a poet of unwritten poems, a wielder of sheathed swords, a lover of my dead mother born again as a young understanding maid and the father by her of men without fear, but when I finish this cup of Irish tea, this cup of stern disillusionment, I shall be merely Denis Dillon, the village schoolmaster, the clerical bell-boy who banks the parochial ha'pence. (*He drains the cup with a mighty gulp and lays it down*) There now, you can spit on me.

PHELIM

(*Touching him softly*)

Come on, Denis, I'll leave you up the road at the school-house.

DILLON

No, I'm not going.

PHELIM

Come on now, like a good lad.

DILLON

No, there's no one there but the ghost of my mother and the cat.

NORA

If you'd had the guts to stick to Dorothy Craig, *she* could be there.

54

DILLON

You're wrong, Nora. When the crisis came and I looked at Dorothy I knew she wasn't mine because I was not prepared to suffer for her. A man must be ready to bear lashes for the woman he loves. I must go on and on until I find the girl that hates me with the hatred of a devil. That girl will be mine.

PHELIM

Don't mind his blatherin'. It's the raw whiskey in his head.

NORA

Liquid bravery. . . .

PHELIM

Come on, Denis.

DILLON

Not yet. Not till I say my say. (*He comes over to her*) How much do you hate me, you fiery little bitch?

NORA

Not more than is healthy. I hate only what is important enough to be hated.

DILLON

If I told you that for giving up Dorothy Craig, I was elected secretary of the Vigilance Committee, how much would you hate me?

NORA

I know all that already. You well deserved the position.

DILLON

If I told you I was out today on duty and that I saw you in a married man's car . . . the car of Michael Shivers, avowed enemy of the new clerical fascism!

PHELIM

(*Alarmed*)

Now, Denis, you saw no such thing!

DILLON

(*Maudlinly*)

As you say, Phelim, I saw no such thing.

NORA

Yes, you did! None of this hiding. It was I!

PHELIM

(*To* NORA)

Can't *you* shut your mouth?

DILLON

That's what I came here for tonight, to warn you. It was the whiskey submerged the good Christian in me and made me charitable and kindly, but when I got here I couldn't remember. It was to tell you, Nora, that the hounds of Banba are on your trail.

PHELIM

You will say nothing of this, I want you to promise me that.

DILLON

I will promise you, Phelim, but in the morning when I stand naked . . . when the whiskey is dead and the sword of Don Quixote gone back to its castle in Spain, what then? I will be Denis Dillon, tell-tale, maker of obeisances and currier of favors. If I could only show you my inside when I am sober! Show you the meanness and the cowardice and the spite. Lord, what an unholy picture I am. Even the cat dislikes me. . . .

NORA

Take him away, Father; he makes me want to kick him.

PHELIM

Here now, pull yourself together and I'll link you up to the schoolhouse. No one will see us. (*He sees a bunch of papers sticking out of* DILLON's *pocket*) And you're losin' things out of your pocket.

NORA

What on earth is that he has there?

PHELIM

It's a whole lot of pages and skulls and crossbones drew on them and "The Man Without Fear" printed under them.

DILLON

(*Seizing the papers and looking at them*)
They're . . . they're not mine. I never saw them before.

PHELIM

They must be yours. They were in your pocket.

DILLON

(*Staring at the papers*)
Yes, I remember now. . . . It was in Shivers's snug down at the waterfront— (*Hoarsely*) Good God, I'm crazy, that's what I am. (*He tears his hair.*)

NORA

What did you do?

DILLON

Nora, for God's sake, go down and ask Shivers did I . . .

NORA

Did you what? Did you do anything agin Shivers?

DILLON

No, not him. He's my friend in secret. Ask him did I give him a letter to slip under a door.

PHELIM

Slip under a door!

DILLON

I think it was that. It must have been to one of that crew on the Vigilance Committee. It was the drink made me brave. I can't remember but I know it was mad of me—mad of me.

PHELIM

Run down, Nora, and see Shivers.

NORA

(*As she crosses*)

Some of these days he will get so brave that he will say boo to Paddy Slaven's goose. (*Turning at the door*) I'm telling Shivers I'm starting work with him in the morning, Father. (PHELIM *shakes his head and* NORA *goes quickly.*)

PHELIM

Can you not think of what you done?

DILLON

(*Defiantly*)

I did nothing . . . nothing! Somebody stuck these drawings in my pocket. You don't believe me. God damn you, do you want me to swear it to you?

58

PHELIM

No, come on and I will lead you home. You will lose your
school, that's what'll happen with your drink.

DILLON

(*With self-pity*)

But sure, the drink is all I have in my life. When I turn the
key in the door and light the paraffin lamp and fasten the
curtains down with drawing pins there's the thrill of shut-
ting them out, the satisfaction of doing something that they
cannot see. Do you understand me, Phelim?

PHELIM

I do not. It's time you were home in bed.

DILLON

Bed . . . that's it . . . another prison and the bones of all
belonging to me musing under the old floors an' cryin' agin
me, and the leaves fallin' agin the windows an' the walls
groaning with the pictures of grim saints. St. Anthony of
Padua, St. Stephen, St. Paul, St. Michael with his foot in your
throttle. There they are, leaning over, leaning down. You fall
asleep by their permission, you dream secretly and at your
peril. When you awaken, there they are, warders jangling
the keys of the eternal puzzle over your head. Good God,
Phelim, can you see me slinking into bed at night without
letting them see that I'm as drunk as the devil?

PHELIM

That's no way to be talkin' of the saints. It's a woman you
want, to take care of you, livin' there alone like an oul' broody
hen.

DILLON

A woman! Do you think I'd have the nerve to take a woman to bed before that crew? (*A knock*) That'll be Nora back, I pray God Shivers didn't slip that letter under a door.

PHELIM

(*Crossing to the door*)
That's not her knock. (*He looks from the window and returns quickly*) It's the priest—the *new* priest.

DILLON

(*Fearfully*)
For God's sake, hide me. . . . No, don't let him in. You can't let him in.

PHELIM

I can't keep the priest out. I'm not come to that yet.

DILLON

I'm lost, that's what I am. (*Gripping* PHELIM) Look at me. Am I all right? Am I drunk? (DILLON *rubs his face with his handkerchief and fixes his hair.*)

PHELIM

(*Straightening him up*)
You're all right. Pull yourself together now. (*A second knock.*)

DILLON

(*Grasping* PHELIM *as he crosses to the door*)
I . . . I was having a general talk about things in the parish. Do you hear me, Phelim?

PHELIM

All right, all right, watch your talk now.

60

DILLON

I will. The drink's dead in me, anyway. I'm Denis Dillon now . . . sober and despicable, the clerical message-boy. (*As* PHELIM *goes to the door,* DILLON *sits down virtuously by the fireside. He is a distressing study in fear, inferiority and inhibition.* PHELIM *comes back followed by* FATHER SHAUGHNESSY *who carries an umbrella and a portfolio of papers. He is composed and shows perfect equanimity.*)

FATHER SHAUGHNESSY

God bless the house, Phelim. (*Seeing* DILLON, *who rises awkwardly*) I see you have Mr. Dillon. A friendly call, Mr. Dillon?

DILLON
(*With an effort*)

Yes, Father, and of course a little bit of a discussion with Phelim about the people and . . . things.

FATHER SHAUGHNESSY

That's good. The little bit extra that means so much. (*As* PHELIM *places a chair for him*) Thank you, Phelim, and how is the care?

PHELIM

If it's Nora you mean, Father, she went down to Shivers's on a message.

DILLON
(*Hurriedly*)

A . . . a . . . couple of cauliflowers Shivers sent up for, Father.

FATHER SHAUGHNESSY

Did she go alone?

61

PHELIM

Sure, it's only down on the sea front, Father.

FATHER SHAUGHNESSY

It's a dark night (*Pause*), and anyway, I dislike this habit of our girls going places alone. It loosens and disintegrates. I wish we could get back to the splendid days in Ireland when our young girls were the stainless jewels of our national heritage.

DILLON

I . . . I offered to accompany her, Father, but she just told me to keep Phelim in chat till she got back.

FATHER SHAUGHNESSY

As the secretary of our Vigilance Committee, Mr. Dillon, you should not *offer* to accompany her; you should *accompany* her.

DILLON

(*Squirming*)

I . . . I stand corrected, Father.

PHELIM

Faith, there's not much use in blamin' the schoolmaster. Nora is none too easy to handle at times.

FATHER SHAUGHNESSY

That explanation, Phelim, does not erase from the Fourth Commandment the words "instruct and correct." I will have a talk with her myself. I am convinced that apart from a little windy froth she has swallowed in England, she's a good girl.

PHELIM

(*Stung a little*)

Froth or no froth, Father, Nora's a good girl.

FATHER SHAUGHNESSY

(*Slowly and calmly*)

That's what I said, Phelim. (*Stiff pause.*)

DILLON

(*Venturingly*)

For my own part, I feel that the trouble with Nora is . . .

PHELIM

(*Blazing out*)

Och, who asked you what you thought about her? Shut up!

DILLON

(*Aghast*)

But, Phelim, I . . .

FATHER SHAUGHNESSY

One moment, Phelim. Mr. Dillon is not now merely the schoolmaster; as an officer in my moral police force in this village, he is, of course, entitled to a much greater respect than before.

PHELIM

(*Morosely*)

I'll not argue with the priest.

DILLON

Sure, I don't think Phelim meant to belittle me, Father.

FATHER SHAUGHNESSY

I am not thinking of *you,* Mr. Dillon. (DILLON *rubs his hot neck with his handkerchief. Pause.* FATHER SHAUGHNESSY *turns to* PHELIM) There's another matter, Phelim, that I wish to discuss with you. It concerns this vegetable account of Canon

63

Lavelle's. (*Pause*) I regret that you thought it necessary in the parochial house to make use of hasty words. You were in a bit of a temper, Phelim. I suppose his temper and his soul are the two things no Irishman will part with.

DILLON
(*Slavishly affecting a laugh*)
His temper and his soul! That's a good one, Father.

FATHER SHAUGHNESSY
I see you find me amusing, Mr. Dillon. (DILLON *hastily freezes and offers to apologize*) No, no, don't apologize. I see no sin in being amusing now and again. (*To* PHELIM) Don't you agree with me, Phelim?

PHELIM
(*Morosely*)
I said I wouldn't argue with the priest, not if I could help it. There's no luck in it.

FATHER SHAUGHNESSY
(*Gravely*)
There's not a bit of harm, Phelim, in arguing with the priest on things that don't matter. (*Pause.*)

PHELIM
I won't say. I will let it be.

FATHER SHAUGHNESSY
You have the gift of silence, Phelim, the gift that loses battles and wins victories.

64

PHELIM
(*Softly*)

It's not our own victories that matter. I can bear defeat for myself at any time, by God's grace, but I . . . I can't bear defeat for the one I love better than myself.

DILLON

He . . . he's worried about Nora, Father.

FATHER SHAUGHNESSY

Quite so! Quite so, but I am certain, Phelim, that will be all right too. (*Pause*) If it doesn't it won't be my fault . . . it won't be for the want of trying.

PHELIM

I am glad to hear that . . . Nora is an orphan at the best.

FATHER SHAUGHNESSY

The Church is also an orphan, Phelim. (*Pause*) But we have got quite away from the vegetables. (*A smile.* DILLON *laughs again affectedly. A knock is heard.*)

DILLON

That's Nora now.

PHELIM

No. That's not her knock. She knocks slow as if she felt the hurt that she mightn't be wanted. (*As he crosses*) That's the knock of a woman that bates her husband. (*He opens the door.* SARAH HEARTY *appears.*)

SARAH

They said at the Chapel House the priest was here.

65

PHELIM

And so he is. Come in. (PHELIM *comes back, followed by* SARAH HEARTY, *who is carrying a letter*) It's Patrick Hearty's woman, Father.

SARAH

(*Excitedly*)

I'm terrible glad you're here, Father. I was in the terror of me life comin' along them dark roads.

FATHER SHAUGHNESSY

You should not be alone, Mrs. Hearty.

SARAH

But Patrick's out on Vigilance duty, Father, and I had to come. Read that.

FATHER SHAUGHNESSY

(*Peering at the lamp*)

I can't read in this light. What is it?

SARAH

It was pushed under my door, Father, after Patrick went out and it gettin' dark.

FATHER SHAUGHNESSY

(*Handing the letter to* DILLON)

Read it for me, Mr. Dillon.

DILLON

(*Shivering, trying to control himself*)

I . . . I'm afraid, Father, my eyes are bad too. I got measured for specs yesterday in Dundooley. I mean examined for glasses.

66

SARAH

I will read it, Father. (*She takes it and holds it up to the light*) "To Mrs. Sarah Hearty. You fermenting big sack of moral barley, ignored by the birds of the air and rejected by Guinness's brewery, keep your wasp's nose to yourself at night or you will get a bullet in the part of you that comes after the rest of you. Signed. The Man Without Fear." (*All stand as if turned to stone.* PHELIM *is horrified.* DILLON, *his eyes secretively on the priest, is a study in fear.* SARAH *is a picture of wronged womanhood.* FATHER SHAUGHNESSY *stands looking out into space grimly. Before the pause finishes, the door opens and* NORA *comes in. She looks at them, nonplussed.* SARAH *quietly hands her the note which she reads slowly. She looks up amazed, then looks down at it again, looks from one to the other and then at* DILLON, *and finally breaks into uncontrollable giggles. All except the* PRIEST *stare at her, horrified. The* PRIEST *does not move from his posture.* DILLON *is in an agony of fear. He gives her looks of cringing appeal and pathetically whispered pleadings.*)

SARAH
(*Outraged*)

I'll bust your jaw for you, you brazen tinker!

PHELIM
(*Moving between them*)

Leave her alone, you! (*To* NORA) Can *you* not have a little sense in you?

FATHER SHAUGHNESSY
(*At length slowly*)

My dear people, this scurrilous outpouring of a mind abandoned to evil is intended to discourage and affright us on our march onwards to the achievement of a new state of things in our little village. All of us except one have been shocked by its indecency. That one has been abroad in a pagan country. We must be painstaking and forbearing until she has learned to re-adjust herself to the Christian State. (NORA *walks round quietly until she is face to face with* FATHER SHAUGHNESSY.)

NORA
(*Staring at him unflinchingly*)
The Christian State! A schoolmaster that scrapes and bows, a father that is afraid of old shadows, a mean stupid old woman and a priest as cold as the mountain stones. (PHELIM *reaches out, takes* NORA *by the arm and jerks her back.*)

PHELIM
(*Firmly*)
That's enough. Not a word more or I'll scatter you!

SARAH
Defyin' the priest. That's what the other side of the water's done for you.

PHELIM
She's not defyin' the priest, Sarah Hearty. Before the oul' Canon lay down on his back did he tell you that you'd make trouble in Heaven and be flung out of it.

SARAH
(*In uproar*)
It's a lie. I'll get Patrick to bate the oul' head off you!

FATHER SHAUGHNESSY
Silence. (*They quieten*) To the scurrilous and the wicked we add bickering and backbiting. Is that our goal? (*Pause*) Mr. Dillon?

68

DILLON

(*Almost jumping*)

Yes, Father.

FATHER SHAUGHNESSY

This wicked note will be entrusted to you as the secretary. (*He hands it to him*) Have you ever seen it before?

DILLON

(*Staring at it*)

I have not, Father. I have not indeed. I . . . I . . . I'm half petrified yet, after hearing it. (*He and* NORA *exchange glances. She secretively spits on the floor before him and he hangs his head.*)

FATHER SHAUGHNESSY

You will leave no stone unturned to find the author of it.

DILLON

I will do my best.

FATHER SHAUGHNESSY

The man . . . or the woman who wrote it is a menace to our very souls. He or she must go. (DILLON *shivers.*)

PHELIM

(*With spirit*)

I don't like the woman part of it, Father. If that's a dig at . . .

FATHER SHAUGHNESSY

I am not concerned with your likes or dislikes, Phelim Fintry. (*Pause*) Nora Fintry, I expect you as a good child to apologize for your unchristian attitude to a scurrilous note. (*Pause.* DILLON *looks uneasily at* NORA.)

PHELIM

You'd be the better of it, Nora. Let you do as the priest wants.

DILLON

(*Coaxing her*)

Your father's right, Nora. I'd do it if I was you. (*They exchange looks and he winces.*)

NORA

But you are not me, you poor mongrel. (*She steps forward*) I will make a bargain with you, Father Shaughnessy.

FATHER SHAUGHNESSY

Bargain! I do not make bargains, child.

NORA

Then I will apologize on one condition.

FATHER SHAUGHNESSY

Condition?

NORA

We shall go together to the Canon and give him this note to read. If, in spite of his pain, he doesn't laugh at it, I will apologize.

SARAH

(*Flaring up*)

Well, I like that, Father! (*Stamping her foot*) The cheek of you, Nora Fintry, you brazen hussy!

FATHER SHAUGHNESSY

Quiet! Quiet!

SARAH

Will you tell me to be quiet, Father, if I tell you that brazen girl there was out nine or ten times in yon Shivers fellow's motor car, a man that misses Mass every second Sunday, and a married man that his wife ran away from.

PHELIM
(*Bursting out*)
That's a lie, a damned lie!

SARAH
That's all you know, Phelim Fintry. How many cuckoos' nests has she built in your ears?

PHELIM
(*Violently*)
Nora, you will explain this to the priest.

NORA
(*Quietly*)
I will explain nothing. (*Pause.*)

FATHER SHAUGHNESSY
Mr. Dillon.

DILLON
Yes, Father.

FATHER SHAUGHNESSY
As the secretary of the Committee, have you official information as to these alleged excursions?

DILLON
Well, there's a certain amount of evidence, Father.

FATHER SHAUGHNESSY
Have you personally witnessed them? (NORA *and* DILLON *exchange glances. Again* DILLON *shivers.* NORA *spits on the floor.*)

DILLON

You see, Father, in my capacity as . . .

FATHER SHAUGHNESSY

I want a yes or no answer, Mr. Dillon. (*Pause.*)

SARAH

Is your precious secretary afraid to tell the truth, Father?

FATHER SHAUGHNESSY

(*Grimly*)

That's still to be seen.

DILLON

(*Painfully*)

I cannot deny, Father, that I saw them a few times but I am
not saying there was anything improper in it.

FATHER SHAUGHNESSY

You're sure as to identity?

DILLON

I'm afraid there can be no doubt as to that.

NORA

Are you also sure, Denis Dillon, you can't identify the
printed writing on that vulgar note written by "The Man
Without Fear"?

DILLON

(*With the courage of fear*)

Your insinuation is a lie, Nora Fintry. I know nothing
about it. I'll swear I don't.

72

PHELIM

(*Catching at her*)

Let him be, Nora.

NORA

(*Staring at him as in a dream*)

Yes, I will let him be.

DILLON

This is very hard, Father, on me.

FATHER SHAUGHNESSY

It is hard for all of us and you will not forget what we said about confusing weakness with pity. We must go on. Make a note, Mr. Dillon, that this matter comes first on the agenda at our meeting tomorrow.

PHELIM

(*Bursting out*)

What are yous goin' to do to my daughter? It's a whole parcel of lies. A conspiracy agin the child.

FATHER SHAUGHNESSY

If it is, Phelim Fintry, we shall not be slow in discovering it.

PHELIM

Yous are wrongin' the child. I'm tellin' yous.

FATHER SHAUGHNESSY

Dare we and meet God! I think not. We too have our souls to keep.

NORA

(*Suddenly breaking out*)

It's true, all true! I may have been born in the bed of a bondsman, but that doesn't make me a thing that creeps. Tomorrow morning, I go to work with Michael Shivers.

73

PHELIM

Stop, Nora, you'll be sorry for this!

FATHER SHAUGHNESSY

I forbid your employment with this man until he receives me in the proper spirit.

NORA

What matter what you forbid! You are agin me anyway and you're agin Shivers. The damned may as well get together.

PHELIM

(*Shaking her*)

You're not to say that! I'll turn you out, do you hear me?

DILLON

(*Coaxingly*)

Nora, would you listen to me if . . .

NORA

Keep back, Denis Dillon. One day I called you a worm. I apologize to that worm; you're a louse. (DILLON *falls back crushed.*)

FATHER SHAUGHNESSY

You will take all this, Mr. Dillon, with the proper humility.

DILLON

Yes, Father.

FATHER SHAUGHNESSY

Nora Fintry, as the servant of God, I am thrice bound to be patient and forbearing.

SARAH

The poor priest! Think shame of yourself, you tinker!

74

FATHER SHAUGHNESSY

I am leaving the door open for you to come tomorrow at five to this meeting and to make before us a good act of humility and a firm resolution not to see this man Shivers again. If you refuse that, direct action must be taken.

PHELIM

I'll answer for her, Father. She'll be there.

FATHER SHAUGHNESSY

I want it from herself.

NORA

I will never be there. I said I was no bondsman's daughter.

FATHER SHAUGHNESSY

The evil you assimilated in a pagan land is deep in you, woman.

NORA

What I have in me that won't let me stoop I didn't get in England, for England hasn't got it to give. I got it here. It was in Aideen when she rode by Oscar's side at the Battle of Garva. It was in Cu Chulainn when he tied himself to a pillar before he'd stoop to death, it was in Ossian when he rode back on Niam's white horse and found the land full of priests like you and little men like that poor schoolmaster there, and it's in me now, making me refuse to come to your council table and swallow the ancient draught of humility. (SARAH HEARTY *suddenly rushes forward and seizes* NORA *in a temper.*)

SARAH

You brazen bitch! Will I stand like this and hear you cheek the priest in my presence with your evil tongue! (*In her*

75

venom she flings NORA *to the ground.* FATHER SHAUGHNESSY *interferes too late.*)

FATHER SHAUGHNESSY
(*To* SARAH)

Keep back! How dare you, woman? (*He bends and gently lifts* NORA *to her feet. She shakes her head to steady herself*) Are you hurt, child? (*They look at each other.*)

NORA
(*Slowly*)

It doesn't matter.

FATHER SHAUGHNESSY

It matters much. (*To* SARAH) Sarah Hearty, for this outrageous act of insubordination, you are summarily dismissed from the Vigilance Committee.

SARAH
(*Protestingly*)

But, Father, this is a terrible thing you are doing!

FATHER SHAUGHNESSY

Go! And at once! (*He points. She goes.*)

SARAH
(*At the door, turning*)

I know what *she* is anyway; a wanton of the English streets, and maybe "The Man Without Fear" and the woman without scruple are one and the same. It could well be. (*She goes.*)

FATHER SHAUGHNESSY
(*Slowly*)

You will all dismiss that from your minds. (*He puts on his hat slowly and prepares to go*) I am leaving you the key of the eternal door, Nora Fintry. The centuries may have rusted your own. (NORA *without looking at him goes off into the bedroom. She is followed quietly by her father. As the* PRIEST *is going, there is a knock.* INSPECTOR TOOMEY *enters and takes off his cap.*)

INSPECTOR TOOMEY

They told me, Father, at the Chapel House that I'd find you here.

FATHER SHAUGHNESSY

What is the matter?

TOOMEY

There's been a serious assault case down at the Stella Maris Hotel owned by Mr. Shivers. The man, Patrick Hearty, forced himself into the licensed premises shortly after closing time and was forcibly ejected by Mr. Shivers.

FATHER SHAUGHNESSY
(*Frowning*)

A very garbled report, indeed. Perhaps, I should say, deliberately garbled. Did Mr. Hearty present his official card on entering?

TOOMEY

So it appears.

FATHER SHAUGHNESSY

Then that was sufficient.

TOOMEY

Mr. Shivers didn't think so.

FATHER SHAUGHNESSY

What Mr. Shivers thinks is not important.

TOOMEY

Maybe so, but the man Hearty has just been taken in a car
to a Dundooley doctor with a broken jaw.

FATHER SHAUGHNESSY

Do you mean as a result of Shivers's violence?

TOOMEY

I do. Mr. Shivers said he had no right of entrance at that
hour and forcibly ejected him.

FATHER SHAUGHNESSY

He was there on my authority.

TOOMEY

So he said, but Shivers said you had no such authority, that
that was for the police.

FATHER SHAUGHNESSY

He will learn otherwise before long.

TOOMEY

Might I remind you, Father, that the only ones with the
right of entry after hours are the police?

FATHER SHAUGHNESSY

How much are they paid not to enter?

TOOMEY

Paid! (*Angrily*) Which of the three of us do you mean?

FATHER SHAUGHNESSY
(*Grimly*)

Each of the three of you.

TOOMEY

I resent that, but I suppose a man in a privileged position like yours can say the like and get off with it.

FATHER SHAUGHNESSY

I will not tolerate impertinence.

TOOMEY

(*Slowly crossing*)

Neither will I tolerate such interference. If I get any of your puffed-up would-be policemen on licensed premises after hours, I will not think twice before charging them with a breach of the law.

FATHER SHAUGHNESSY

I will deal with such an exigency when it arises. In the meantime I advise you . . .

TOOMEY

I will be advised only by my superior officers. My duty now is to tell you that the man Hearty thinks he has a case and is charging Mr. Shivers with assault.

FATHER SHAUGHNESSY

Quite right.

TOOMEY

Right or wrong, you will be called as a witness.

FATHER SHAUGHNESSY

That will give me great pleasure in view of Mr. Hearty's official position in my Vigilance Committee. I shall press for an exemplary fine.

TOOMEY
(*As he goes off*)
If that's the law, I'm an idiot.

FATHER SHAUGHNESSY
(*Grimly*)
No one, I am sure, will dispute that contention. (*The* IN-
SPECTOR *slams on his cap and goes off.* DILLON *comes forward
uneasily*) You have heard, Mr. Dillon.

DILLON
I have, every word, Father.

FATHER SHAUGHNESSY
Scurrilous letters, now violence, but we must not be dis-
couraged. We must go on steadily.

DILLON
I suppose that is the law of doing difficult things.

FATHER SHAUGHNESSY
You will attend with me at the court on this assault. If we
win it, it will be like the fire on the hill of Slane kindled
again. We *must* win it.

DILLON
It will be a recognition of the moral policeman, Father.

FATHER SHAUGHNESSY
And more, much more. (*As he crosses*) And McGiolla
Phadraig is a good friend. (*He goes off.* DILLON *stares after
him, then turns and walks slowly to the fireside. He sits down
heavily and morosely buries his head in his hands.* PHELIM *and*
NORA *come in pensively from the bedroom.*)

PHELIM

(*Talking as he enters*)

So you see how it is, child. Arguin' never done any good. No man livin' or dead in this country ever got the better of them. The policeman we can always shoot down, but the priest we must always leave to God and God is always too slow for the old venom that is in us. (*Pause*) Nora, will you go back to England now?

NORA

I've already told you, Father, that I am staying where I belong.

PHELIM

You will fight it out.

NORA

Yes, I will defend what is mine. Someone will have to do it sometime.

PHELIM

I don't want to be hard on you, Nora, but you can't be agin the priest here with me. It's agin my conscience and everything that's in me.

NORA

I will have to sleep in, in Shivers's Hotel, anyway. That will make it easy for you to disown me.

PHELIM

That's not the fair thing to say to a father.

NORA

All right, then, Father, let us leave it unsaid, as if it wasn't there.

PHELIM

Enemies . . . making enemies all the time. Now even your own father is an enemy. (*He wanders across the stage, wor-*

ried) I will dodge up and see the old Canon. Maybe he'd give me a grip again of the old things I knew. (*Pause*) Will I tell him you were asking for him?

NORA

Do!

PHELIM

You remember how he used to call you Noreen. He used to say, "You are too serious, Noreen. Let you leap over your own shadow and you'll hear fairy music," but you'd rather sit on the window sill longin' to be Niam on her white steed.

NORA

Yes! My white steed. (*She looks out in front of her, hidden emotion filling her eyes and face*) How I would watch for it coming down from the fairy path and over the stream in Paddy Slaven's field. . . . Then one day the old packman that used to come on Fridays told me he saw·it being sold by a little black man at the fair of Mullacrew. . . . And after that I . . . I felt the hate in me of all things black and little . . . (*Her voice breaks. There is a long pause*) Don't charge the Canon that account for the vegetables, Father. There's no use in hurting an old man.

PHELIM

Sure, it was just a puff of the bad temper in me. I'll let it be. (*As he goes*) God help me, and I with a daughter that's like a strange woman to me. (*He goes off.* NORA *looks out in front as if in a dream.*)

NORA

Niam and her white steed . . . "And when she looked on Ossian and saw how wise and tender he was and how beautiful and strong, she felt herself filled with a great love for him and longingly and with quiet hands, she drew the folds of her robe of gold more closely to her and made room for him behind her on the back of the white steed." (NORA *looks down at the miserable form of* DILLON, *his head still morosely in his hands*) Well, "Man Without Fear," are you going home tonight?

DILLON

Why do you call me that?

NORA

Isn't that what you call yourself?

DILLON

Only when I'm drunk.

NORA

You poor devil.

DILLON
(*Lifting his head slowly*)
Look at me, Nora. Amn't I a miserable, despicable creature? If you could see the inside of me.

NORA

What do you want me to do, pity you?

DILLON
(*Almost sobbing*)
Give me one little word of sympathy, I need it. (*Pause.*)

NORA
(*Looking at him*)
God forgive me. My only impulse is to kick you. (*Sudden passion seizes her*) Get up and get out of here before I murder you. Go on, get out! Get out! Get out!

83

DILLON

(*Rising and cowering away from her*)

Yes, I will . . . I will go. Just give me a minute to . . . to collect myself. God, the eyes you have! Pitiless, ruthless. You could strip me and flog me, couldn't you?

NORA

(*Between her teeth*)

Yes! Yes! Lay weals on you!

DILLON

Only a disappointed virgin could be like you, vicious and merciless. If you were a woman, you would have taken my head and given me a little word.

NORA

You little devil! You are shrewd, for all your cowardliness.

DILLON

All cowards are shrewd. If only I was drunk I could tell you more. I could tell you much more. It's not for nothing I lie over the gutterin' candle at night and drink and read when my holy master is in bed in the Chapel House. Little does he know that I can rock his rafters with Rabelais and break whiskey glasses with Boccaccio. And you lying in bed riding over the billows on your white steed away from King and Pope and the little men and their priests. Are we not a little like each other, after all? When I am drunk with whiskey and you are drunk with dreams, are we not the hidden Ireland the poets in Dublin never write about; the wandering ghosts of what was there when the priests and the little men came in from the seas? (*Pause. They look at each other.*)

84

NORA

(*Softly*)

Maybe you're right, Denis. Maybe we *are* a little like each other.

DILLON

(*Pathetically grasping her two hands*)

Nora, thank you! Thank you for sayin' that. Oh, how much, how very much that means to me. (NORA *brings her hand slowly to his head and touches his hair.*)

NORA

There! Was that what you wanted?

DILLON

Yes, it lifts me up, like the drink, out of the grave. It is all strange and terrible. When you spat on the floor tonight when I betrayed you, I knew in a flash that I would love you to the end of everything. (*Sobbing*) Don't send me away out where I will be a little black man again, weeding the clerical garden. Lift me on your white steed, Nora.

NORA

Every man, Denis, must lift himself on the white steed.

DILLON

That's what I fear and dread. That's why I will never escape, never! I have come out of the Firbolgs. . . . I have come out of the little men that Ossian found in the place of Finn. Help me, Nora!

NORA

What do you want me to do, Denis?

85

DILLON

I want to have courage. I want to break down this fear that is in me. To be able to look at men, even at my masters and not shiver with the cold.

NORA

But in the morning, it will be different. When they say "come" to you, you will come, and when they say "go" to you, you will go.

DILLON

It's true. From the moment I rise, I go in fear. When I look up at the dark saints over my bed, when I look out of the window and see the priest's house and when I turn my key in the school door. And all my leisure is spent in dreamin' of things burnin', of things fallin', of things I see myself smashin'. And look at me, look well at me! (*Pause.*)

NORA

I have always loved the smashing of things too, since I was a little girl. Look, Denis, like you with your saints, I have suffered these cups for months past; they're coarse and thick and stupid and callous, and I hate the sight of them because they hurt me. Let's smash them into smithereens. (*They look at each other.*)

DILLON

You're crazy! Phelim would be ragin' mad!

NORA

I knew you'd say just that. (*She hurls a cup against the wall and smashes it*) There! (*She smashes another one*) And there! (*He looks at her fascinated, rushes across, seizes a cup and throws it.*)

DILLON

And there!

NORA

(*Smashing*)

And there!

DILLON

(*Smashing*)

And there!

NORA

(*Smashing*)

And there!

DILLON

(*Smashing*)

And there! It's wonderful. I feel as if there was the taste of blood in my mouth, the taste of the blood of my enemies, the taste of the blood of the scoundrels who have taught me to love their laws and hate life. I, that have warm blood and the laugh of a giant. (*He laughs in abandonment, then suddenly he pauses and is quiet. He and* NORA *stare at each other bright-eyed and flushed, then with a cry they come to each other wordlessly. They are clasped in each other's arms passionately, as the* CURTAIN FALLS.)

Curtain

ACT THREE

ACT THREE

SCENE I

*The sitting room of the Parochial House, as in Act One. A
week later.*

CANON LAVELLE *is asleep, in the chair, his head on the pillow.
He is breathing heavily.*

ROSIEANNE *and* MEG MC GHEE, *the latter a comparatively
young red-headed tartish servant, brought down by* FATHER
SHAUGHNESSY, *are both dusting. They are bitterly antagonistic
to each other. When* MEG *dusts a piece of furniture,* ROSIEANNE
*follows and dusts it all over again. They give each other con-
stant fiery glances.*

MEG
(*Angrily*)

I dusted that.

ROSIEANNE
(*Angrily*)

An' *I'm* dustin' it again.

MEG

If you don't watch your step, I'll dust your face for you.

ROSIEANNE

Go on and try, Carrots.

91

MEG

(*Passionately countering*)

Why, you withered oul' bag of bones . . . (*Their hands get into each other's hair and they start tearing and panting heavily. The* CANON *starts in his sleep and mutters.*)

CANON

(*Sleepily*)

From lightning and tempest, O Lord, deliver us. I—I— (*He yawns*) Hey, Rosieanne, are you there, Rosieanne? (*They stop their quarrel secretively.* ROSIEANNE *adjusts her hair and dress and crosses.*)

ROSIEANNE

(*Sweetly*)

Oh, you're wakened again, Canon. That was a grand sleep you had.

CANON

It was no grand sleep at all, and I'm half starved anyway. Is there no tea in the house?

ROSIEANNE

I'll bring it in to you as soon as I get in some milk. The Widow Whelan stopped sendin' up the milk and the home-made butter.

CANON

She—she what?

ROSIEANNE

She did, Canon. Father Shaughnessy refused yesterday to baptise her daughter's child; her that married the Protestant that has the mowin' machine and the threshin' mill, an' she's vowin' vengeance. Never again, she says, will one in this house as much as smell her butter or drink her milk.

CANON
(*Woefully*)

That—that's the worse news yet, Rosieanne, and never a penny did she charge me once.

ROSIEANNE

It's that oily American butter that's in the shops, Canon, an' a smell off it that would turn a hearse back.

CANON
(*Vexed*)

Och, what's the use of me tryin' to get the better of paralysis if I'm goin' to die of woeful want and starvation anyway? Is Father Shaughnessy back yet?

ROSIEANNE

He's in at the court case in Dundooley, Canon, that Shivers is up at, for breaking Patrick Hearty's jaw bone.

CANON

It's not his jaw bone I'd break if I had my paws on him. There I am now, without a bit of cauliflower or a saucepan of milk that's not half water, or a bit of the widow's butter that even dead men dream about. (*Pause*) Is there anything at all I can have to my tea?

ROSIEANNE

When I'm out for the milk I'll buy you a fruit cake in Gogarty's with cloves and raisins in it.

CANON

Be quick then, an' if you stop for a blather with anyone, don't forget all about me.

ROSIEANNE

I won't even talk to myself, I'll be that quick. (*She goes hurriedly.* MEG *dusts her way over to the* CANON.)

MEG

(*Sweetly*)

Are you any better, Canon?

CANON

(*Looking sideways at her*)

Sure, I'm not sick at all, only me legs won't—won't stand.

MEG

It's a shame you havin' to ate them oul' shop-made pies. Sure, it's the scrapin's of the counter they make *them* with, and beetles and flies and spiders all mixed up in them.

CANON

(*Wryly speaking*)

Is—is that true?

MEG

Troth an' it's true, Canon. (*Pause*) That's the best of being able always to do your own bakin'. I was trained to bake when I was in England. (*Pause*) I'm just after makin' a grand plate of hot muffins for Father Shaughnessy's tea. Sure, I'll just bring you in a few of them, Canon, with a cup of hot tea.

CANON

(*Struggling*)

Well—it would be grand, surely, but better not, Meg. I don't want any quarrelling with Rosieanne.

MEG

Sure, just as you say, Canon. (*Pause*) They have a strawberry center with cream on top and a facing of fresh jam.

CANON

(*Swallowing*)

Do you tell me that! They must be—be game ball.

MEG

Sure, I wouldn't be a minute, Canon.

CANON

Go— Go on, then, in the name of God, but don't let her see you now.

MEG

(*Triumphantly*)

Just give me a minute, Canon. Sure, what she won't know won't sicken her. (*She rushes off, left. The* CANON *sits up, evidently ill at ease. He cocks his ear and listens now and again, scratches his head, etc.* FATHER SHAUGHNESSY *enters, right, and flings down his hat. He looks flushed and triumphant.*)

FATHER SHAUGHNESSY

Are you sleeping, Canon?

CANON

No, but I'm half starved. Did you hear that the Widow Whelan is sendin' up no more of her grand butter and creamy milk?

FATHER SHAUGHNESSY

(*With a deprecatory wave*)

Trifles!—trifles! . . . What is more important is that this day at the courts we have struck a great blow for Ireland.

CANON

Och, great blows have been gettin' struck for Ireland since I was the size of a drumstick an' we're still livin' on spuds and buttermilk.

FATHER SHAUGHNESSY

These were the blows of politicians, men of froth and egotism. This is new and different. We have won our case, Canon, and this man Shivers was fined five guineas or thirty days. Do you know what that means?

CANON

It means a fine big hole in all our future quarterly collections.

FATHER SHAUGHNESSY

It means the State recognition of our Parochial Vigilance Committees—a new army of policemen who will steer this nation back to its Catholic heritage. Tomorrow, moral committees like ours will be functioning in every parish. That, Canon, is our solution of all the problems of youth in Ireland.

CANON

Och, you're imagin' things. You should have been a Presbyterian clergyman born in Scotland and brought up on oatcakes and Calvinism. When I was a young whipper before I got the call to the Church, I kissed me girl at the cross roads, aye, and walloped Jeremiah Duggan on the public road for tryin' to do the same. That same girl since gave a son to the Easter rising, and a daughter to the Carmelites. It's not bad for what you'd call a brazen woman. (*Enter* MEG, *left, with tray containing cup of tea and hot muffins.*)

96

FATHER SHAUGHNESSY

Canon, these disclosures of yours are not—theologically dignified.

CANON

Well, here's hopin' God's no theologian or we'll all get our backsides scorched. I'd rather a pennyworth of old Mary Cassidy's faith. (*Smelling muffins*) My, that's a brave an' fine smell, Meg.

MEG

I have put a wee bit of extra jam on the tops, Canon.

CANON

I can see that, Meg. You're a genius. I always heard it said that red-heads made the worst of friends and the best of cooks.

MEG

Thank you, Canon. I will see in future you get good hot cookin' an' nice tasty bakin'.

CANON

Yes, but—but don't fight now with Rosieanne.

MEG

I'll not fight, Canon, if *she* doesn't.

CANON
(*Dubiously*)

That's cold comfort, I'm afraid.

MEG

Will I bring *your* tea, Father?

FATHER SHAUGHNESSY

Not for an hour. I have work to do yet.

MEG

But the muffins will be cold, Father.

FATHER SHAUGHNESSY

The muffins are not important.

MEG

Very well, Father. (*She goes off, left, hurt.*)

CANON

Could you not please the craythur an' praise her muffins? Sure, they're grand.

FATHER SHAUGHNESSY

Meg should know me better by this.

CANON

As if a red-head ever knew better. Isn't that the grand thing about them!

FATHER SHAUGHNESSY
(*Testily*)

I wish you'd let me get those papers straight for our Committee, Canon.

CANON

Oh, go ahead with your spiritual ledgers, but I still believe God's a poet. My, that's a darling muffin. I hope it doesn't start talkin' back to me later on. (FATHER SHAUGHNESSY *shifts irritably*) Do you ever notice our girshes are never worth a rap at anything until they spend a few years in England.

FATHER SHAUGHNESSY

I don't believe it, but if it's true, we will change that too. (*He continues working and checking.*)

CANON

If I was young again I'd take the faith of the people for granted and I'd get all the girshes round me an' form classes on bakin' an' cookin' and on how to get rid of the big savage dish of spuds in the center of the table an' how to get the real nourishment out of our food instead of throwin' the best of it to the cattle like they're doin' now.

FATHER SHAUGHNESSY
(*Testily*)

Canon, please! . . . (CANON *looks at him and stops.* ROSIE-ANNE *enters, left. The* CANON *guiltily pushes away the tea tray.*)

ROSIEANNE

I have the milk, Canon, and a grand fruit cake with raisins and . . . (*She stops suddenly, looks at the tea tray, then at the* CANON, *and finally bursts into tears and starts crying in a highly pitched childish way. The* CANON *looks at her helplessly.* FATHER SHAUGHNESSY *stares at her with a face of thunder.*)

CANON
(*Lamely*)

There now, Rosieanne, there now— I—I got a sudden woeful pain in me leg an' I . . .

FATHER SHAUGHNESSY
(*Angrily*)

What on earth is that yelping for? Get out of here.

ROSIEANNE

I'm leavin', I'm leavin', Canon, I'm leavin' this minute. I'll not stay another second. (*She goes, left, still crying noisily.*)

99

CANON

Whisht now, whisht. You're not goin' one step. I can explain all. I can . . . (*He works the wheels of his chair and sails out after her, gesticulating.*)

FATHER SHAUGHNESSY
(*Sitting down heavily*)

Will nobody rid me of this old gourmant? (MEG *enters briskly.*)

MEG

This is Mr. Shivers of the Stella Maris Hotel to see you, Father. (SHIVERS *appears at the door. He is a big, thick-set man, coarse but capable of very generous impulses if taken the right way. He eyes* FATHER SHAUGHNESSY *with sullen defiance.*)

FATHER SHAUGHNESSY
(*Surprised but steadying himself*)

Good afternoon.

MEG

Beggin' your pardon, Father, may I ask again about the tea?

FATHER SHAUGHNESSY
(*Grimly*)

Haven't I already told you about that?

MEG

But it's me—me lovely muffins, Father, goin' to loss in the oven.

FATHER SHAUGHNESSY
(*Fiercely*)

Bring the muffins to me here. (*She bows and goes, left.* FATHER SHAUGHNESSY *turns to* SHIVERS) You may sit over here,

Mr. Shivers, I will attend to you in a moment if you will excuse me.

SHIVERS
(*Crossing and sitting offhandedly*)

It's all right with me. (*As* SHIVERS *sits,* MEG *knocks and brings in a tray of steaming muffins. She's half afraid but yet still proud of her art.*)

MEG

This is them, Father. Sure, it's a sin to have them gettin' hard and lumpy. (FATHER SHAUGHNESSY *calmly takes the tray across, opens the window, back, pitches the muffins out of it and returning calmly with the empty tray.*)

FATHER SHAUGHNESSY
(*Handing* MEG *the tray*)

Now, that's to teach you a lesson. That's to show you that none of these things is important—that nothing is important but the work I have in hand. Now get outside and let me get on with it.

MEG
(*In a low voice, the tears in her eyes*)

Yes, Father. (*She turns with the tray, crushed in spirit and pride and goes subduedly.* FATHER SHAUGHNESSY *turns, adjusts some papers and addressing himself without any sign of passion or ruffled feelings to* MR. SHIVERS.)

FATHER SHAUGHNESSY

And now, Mr. Shivers, my apologies for keeping you waiting, but these matters of discipline are of great importance.

SHIVERS

(With a shrug)

I don't agree with throwin' fine bakin' out of a window.
I have had to send to England to get a girl for my hotel that
can bake like that girl, but of course it's no business of mine.

FATHER SHAUGHNESSY

Of course it isn't; and now, what can I do for you?

SHIVERS

I am here to discuss a few matters with you.

FATHER SHAUGHNESSY

Good. To agree to discuss matters is always half a battle.
Well now?

SHIVERS

Don't mistake me. (*He places his hat on the table and faces*
FATHER SHAUGHNESSY *squarely*) Father Shaughnessy, you know
as well as me that McGiolla Phadraig's ruling in court today
that Patrick Hearty had the right to enter my hotel after hours
is the ruling of a jackass.

FATHER SHAUGHNESSY

On that, Mr. Shivers, I regret I cannot agree with you.

SHIVERS

(Tapping table)

Very well, Father. The only course open to me now is to
defend my premises with all the means at my disposal.

FATHER SHAUGHNESSY

(Rising, as they confront each other)

There have been men in every country who have always re-
sisted the pioneers. History shows us that such men have al-

ways been blasted out of the way. I will say no more than that.

SHIVERS

You have said enough. (*As they stare at each other, there is a knock, and* INSPECTOR TOOMEY *comes in.*)

TOOMEY

A word with you, Father Shaughnessy.

FATHER SHAUGHNESSY
(*After a pause*)

Proceed.

TOOMEY

You are acquainted with the girl Nora Fintry.

FATHER SHAUGHNESSY

I am. She is one of my parishioners.

TOOMEY

Before being one of your parishioners, she is a citizen of this State with full citizen papers, and she has appealed to me for protection against your Vigilance Committee.

FATHER SHAUGHNESSY

The sequence is not important.

TOOMEY

To me the sequence is very important. It determines whether she has or has not the right to secular independence.

SHIVERS

There's the damn thing I've been tryin' to say, and I hadn't the schoolin' to put it in words. I demand your protection, too. (*A pause.* TOOMEY *regards* FATHER SHAUGHNESSY.)

SHIVERS

(*Impatiently to* TOOMEY)

Well? How long more are you going to stand there silent before the priest?

TOOMEY

As long as I feel I can get a peaceful decision. As a man that's been through raids and ambushes with the flying squads in the revolution racket, I know what hate and venom are. I know what it feels like to want to tear the guts out of an enemy. I know what it is to shoot down men at point-blank range out of a sense of duty. That sense of duty is my ruling passion. Do you know now why I'm standing here without a word?

FATHER SHAUGHNESSY

Do I understand that you are threatening *me,* Inspector Toomey?

TOOMEY

(*Grimly*)

I've never threatened a man in my life. Threats are an evasion of duty, and I never evade my duty.

FATHER SHAUGHNESSY

Do you recognize that I too have a strong sense of duty?

TOOMEY

Of course I do, Father Shaughnessy.

FATHER SHAUGHNESSY

Then need we be opposed?

TOOMEY

That is for you to say. I don't want to quarrel with you if I can help it. We both have the dirty work to do, and nobody ever thanks us for it. Everyone has a bad word for both of us in the end. Why should we quarrel? You stick to your pulpit, and I'll stick to my barracks. What are they, after all, but the two strait-jackets of human nature!

FATHER SHAUGHNESSY

You forget one important thing in giving me advice, Inspector Toomey.

TOOMEY

And that?

FATHER SHAUGHNESSY

I never asked for it. I have work to do here and I will do it. Tomorrow the rest of Ireland will be doing exactly what I am doing. I am convinced of that.

TOOMEY

Take it or leave it. Come along, Shivers. You and Nora Fintry have certain secular rights under the common law, and it's my job here to see they're protected. (TOOMEY *moves towards the door.* SHIVERS *follows him out.*)

FATHER SHAUGHNESSY
(*As they go*)
This has gone far enough. It's time the Ministry of Justice in Dublin knew of your impertinences. (*As they exchange glances,* FATHER SHAUGHNESSY *sits down peremptorily at the desk and starts to write a letter. As he writes,* CANON LAVELLE *wheels himself in.*)

CANON

If you're not busy, Father Shaughnessy, I'll turn on the radio to hear if Jeremiah Mulligan knocked out that black man from the wilds of America, God help us.

105

FATHER SHAUGHNESSY
(*Curtly*)

I'm writing an important letter.

CANON
(*Resigned*)

Aw, well; sure he'll knock him out anyway with God's help. They say he blesses himself before every round.

FATHER SHAUGHNESSY
(*Irascibly*)

Please! Please! (*The* CANON *with a sigh subsides.* NORA FINTRY *knocks and enters carrying a small basket.*)

NORA

Canon, my father sent these to you. They are the fresh lettuce and the young cauliflowers you sent down for.

CANON
(*Aroused*)

Sure, Lord, Nora, I was just lyin' dreamin' about them. (*He takes the basket*) Sit down, child, and blather to me for awhile.

NORA
(*Seeing* FATHER SHAUGHNESSY)

Some other time, Canon, I must be going now.

CANON
(*Sadly*)

Please don't go, Nora. Sure nobody comes laughin' to me now at all, and I get lonely for the young faces. . . . (*Yearningly*) I—I knew your mother, Nora . . . and your grannie. . . . Sure I was mad about your grannie when I was a boy.

She used to wear one of them wee frilly bonnets over her gold hair and Lord, you could hear her petticoats swishing a mile away. . . . Will ye not sit down, child?

NORA
(Tenderly)
I can't. . . . Don't think hard of me, Canon.

CANON
I think hard of no one, Nora. What right have I to? When I feel a distaste for someone I remember that God in His wisdom made them so. I wish the whole sad world could put away all their great knowledge and learn just that much.

NORA
I wish they could, Canon.

FATHER SHAUGHNESSY
(Rising and crossing)
Have you come to see me too, Nora Fintry?

NORA
(Turning gently)
I can't say in truth that I have, Father Shaughnessy.

FATHER SHAUGHNESSY
(Humanly)
No matter. Perhaps you *will* come, later on.

NORA
It is hardly likely.

FATHER SHAUGHNESSY
Poor child, to be so tormented. . . . Then to show you the difference in our spirits, *I* shall come to see *you*. (*They look*

at each other) There now! (*Magnanimously*) I have decided to have you reinstated in your position in the library, on two conditions.

CANON

Thanks be to God.

NORA
(*Slowly*)

There must be *no* conditions. . . . (*They regard each other, visibly stiffening.*)

CANON
(*Appeal*)

Sure let yous not be hard on each other. Doesn't God love the two of yous without weighin' and measurin'?

FATHER SHAUGHNESSY

You prefer defiance?

NORA
(*Softly*)

What *is* defiance? If it is the struggle of a spirit to escape standardization and to preserve its integrity and humanity, then I *am* defiant. But I am not alone. The broken heart of humanity is defiant too, today. (*Breaking suddenly into tears*) Oh, God, can't you see? Can't you see?

FATHER SHAUGHNESSY
(*In sudden temper*)

I can see nothing but a proud and intractable woman whom I will not tolerate as a living scandal in our midst. (*They are facing each other defiantly, the tears glistening in* NORA's *eyes, and* FATHER SHAUGHNESSY's *face cold as chiselled steel, when* DENIS DILLON *knocks and enters.*)

108

DILLON
(*Nervously*)
You—sent for me, Father Shaughnessy? I—I didn't know Nora was here. (*Seeing her tears*) Why, you're crying, Nora. (*They look at each other strangely.* DILLON's *eyes glisten angrily for a second. He puts out a hand to her courageously and she suddenly comes to his shoulder and sobs.*)

CANON
Take her home, Denis, like a good boy. She—she's a wee bit upset.

FATHER SHAUGHNESSY
Then you will return here instantly. I have work for you.

DILLON
(*Rebellious for a second, then submissive*)
Very well.

NORA
(*Looking at him, without reproach*)
Poor Denis. Some day you will be strong enough to say what must be said. (PATRICK HEARTY *enters.*)

HEARTY
Sorry I'm a little late, Father. You have work for me?

FATHER SHAUGHNESSY
I have. Work for both of you.

DILLON
Come, Nora. I'll leave you down, if you'll—walk with me. (*His head is down. He avoids her eyes.*)

NORA

(*As she takes his arm forbearingly*)

Never mind, Denis. Some day the dark saints will fall—all over the world. (*They go off together. The* CANON *looks after them sadly.* FATHER SHAUGHNESSY *and* HEARTY *regard each other grimly.*)

CANON

(*As if to himself*)

The poor children . . . It's a terrible thing in a nation when the young are unhappy. . . . (*Looking at* HEARTY) Well, Hearty, you big ass, is it true you took the pledge forever?

HEARTY

It is, Canon.

CANON

God help us. I once knew a man like you that took the pledge, and he murdered his wife. . . .

FATHER SHAUGHNESSY

Canon, these drivellings of yours are unfortunate. In spite of them, we must essentially have obedience and discipline and rules.

CANON

Aye, so the wise men of the world say. But look at the world. . . . Thank God, I'm still stupid and foolish enough to prefer a young smile. But, like Christ, I'm casting my pearls. . . . I could be better occupied. I'll eat my lettuce. (*He takes a large piece of lettuce and starts munching it.* FATHER SHAUGHNESSY *gives him a long look, exclaims with disgust and turns to* HEARTY *with grim resolve.*)

FATHER SHAUGHNESSY
(Gravely)

Mr. Hearty, you know of the defiant and outrageous attitude of this girl Nora Fintry. We are now in the grave position that we have no alternative but direct action. (*He rises gravely, tapping the table with his pencil*) That girl must be broken. (*Passionately*) We must make an example of her, an example that will be the acid test of our determination, an example that by God's grace will be speedily followed all over Ireland. (*Turning*) Our moral law is the only legitimate law in this land or in any land. Go out, on my authority, get Dillon and my men together and when you find this girl publicly associating with this married man Shivers, bring her here before me.

HEARTY
(Breathlessly)

By—by what means, Father?

FATHER SHAUGHNESSY
(Almost in a whisper, tensely)

By the only means that is left to us. (HEARTY, *full of grim resolve, with a long look at* FATHER SHAUGHNESSY, *goes.* FATHER SHAUGHNESSY *goes to the table and stands pensively, his fist clenched, his face grim. He lifts up his head slightly.*)

CANON
(From the chair)

That's the maddest order that was ever given, since the charge of the Light Brigade. You had a right to consult the Bishop first.

FATHER SHAUGHNESSY
(*Angrily*)

The Bishop is an old man, as you are an old man. The moral law of this country must be exalted by someone with sufficient moral courage, otherwise what is the use in our having a new Christian constitution?

CANON

The only thing you will exalt is the question whether the priest is or is not above the civil law. A nice how-do-you-do there will be then. And every shrewd churchman from Donegal to Dingle will call you a blunderin' ass.

FATHER SHAUGHNESSY

Tch! I am tired of your inanities. I am going to put down my foot in *your* case also and insist on your going to a home for old men. (*He goes out with an impatient wave. The* CANON *jumps about in the chair explosively.*)

CANON

A—a—a home for old men! The cheek of him! The—the damned cheek of him!

Curtain

ACT THREE

Scene 2

The same as in the previous scene. The same evening.
The CANON *is sitting shuffling about irascibly in the invalid's chair.*
ROSIEANNE *is sitting knitting by him. A folded paper is lying near a small table.*
The CANON *lifts his head decisively.*

CANON
(*Persistently*)
I'm sure I could stand, Rosieanne.

ROSIEANNE
(*Pushing the* CANON *back*)
But you can't, Canon. I'm tellin' you.

CANON
But I feel it in me.

ROSIEANNE
Now you only imagine that. You'd fall and hurt your spine.
The doctor warned me.

CANON
Heavens! Is there nobody left in the wide world that has
any faith either in the Blessed Mother or in himself.

113

ROSIEANNE

Now, faith is all right in the chapel, but the doctor's the doctor.

CANON

Och, that fellow would make people believe the sparrows were sittin' cooin' on me tombstone. If I was only just riz, Rosieanne! Rebellion in every face and not as much of the grace of God left in the place as would sit on a threepenny bit. (*Pause*) Stop that knittin' when I'm talkin' to you.

ROSIEANNE

But sure it's a new pair of warm socks for vourself I'm doin' an' them oul' ones on you all holes.

CANON

Och, I hate oul' women at any time but when they knit they're more than blood can bear.

ROSIEANNE

(*Putting down her knitting*)
What do you want me to do then, Canon?

CANON

(*Throwing down his rug*)
I'm gettin' on me props! Out of me way!

ROSIEANNE

(*Pressing him back*)
Canon, please listen to me. You can't walk, you know you can't.

CANON

I can, I know I can. The Mother of God will let me walk. When I was dozing today I gave her a right straight talkin' to.

ROSIEANNE

Canon! That's a terrible thing to say.

CANON

Not a bit. She knows rightly I have the divil's own temper when I'm riz'. Here, hold me arm. (*He starts to rise.*)

ROSIEANNE

(*Holding tightly to him*)

God protect you, since you won't do what I tell you. (CANON *lurches forward and collapses in a heap on the floor.* ROSIE-ANNE *looks down at him in tears*) God help you! Will you listen to me now?

CANON

Lift me back, Rosieanne. (*She catches him under the shoulders and with much grunting and groaning succeeds in replacing him in his former position*) As much as one word out of you now, an' I'll give you five second's notice.

ROSIEANNE

I'm not sayin' a word.

CANON

(*Testily*)

It would answer you better if you'd go and get me somethin' to eat, an' not have me half starved.

ROSIEANNE

Half starved? Only an hour ago you got a bowl of broth an' two whole wood pigeons.

CANON

Aye, faith, an' the belly shot out of the two of them. I want tea an' toast.

ROSIEANNE

The toast will be dry. You said you wanted no more of that American shop butter.

CANON

(*Woefully*)

So I did. Can you not coax yon Widow Whelan to bring me up some of her grand butter the same as she used to?

ROSIEANNE

How can I? That child of her daughter's is not baptised yet—her that married the Protestant with the mowin' machine.

CANON

It beats all! (*Whisperingly*) Away down, Rosieanne, an' tell the Widow Whelan to slip up with the child an' I'll get a drop of water an' baptise it meself in the bathroom. (*As* ROSIEANNE *rises in wonderment*) And tell her to stick a—a— pound or two of her butter under her oxter when she's comin', as an offering.

ROSIEANNE

But Father Shaughnessy will report you to the Bishop for interferin', an' I know it's me will get all the blame.

CANON

What does it matter who's blamed or reported in the end? Go on now, go on, in the name of God. (ROSIEANNE *goes. He wriggles irascibly in the chair*) If only I could rise! (*His head down*) I'm a wicked oul' spawn, that's what I am. No wonder she flopped me on the floor when I thought I could walk. (MICHAEL SHIVERS *knocks and enters.*)

SHIVERS

Can I have a word with you, Canon?

CANON

An' since when, Michael, have you to ask leave for that?

SHIVERS

(*With a shrug*)

Och, sure, the times that's in it. . . . Listen, Canon. There's a bust-up coming. (MEG MC GHEE *enters with a feather duster.*)

MEG

Would I be disturbin' you, Canon, if I was to dust the chairs?

CANON

Arrah, you'll dust your red head off some of these days, Meg. Away an' give the dust a rest.

MEG

Oh, if it is that I'm in your way, Canon. (*As she retreats, the* CANON *sniffs.*)

CANON

That's a grand smell, Meg. Some of these days a man'll run away with you. (*To* SHIVERS) She's the grandest cook in the country, Michael.

SHIVERS

If she is, it may be news to her to know I'm sending to England tonight for a fancy baker for the hotel: £6 a month, free board and a nice room and plenty of chances of getting one of them American tourists that suffer from dyspepsia and rye whiskey.

MEG

(*Cajolingly*)

Please, Mr. Shivers, could I get a trial with you?

CANON

What's that!

117

SHIVERS

What about His Eminence, Father Shaughnessy?

MEG

Sure, he never appreciated my bakin' anyway. Sure, you might as well be bakin' strawberry tarts and apple fritters for the stone statue of Wolf Tone in the Square.

SHIVERS

All right then, if you want a chance; but keep that hair of yours out of the dough.

MEG

(*Eagerly*)

I'll pack this minute and be down the next minute. I have let the grass grow under my feet long enough. (*She goes, left, hilariously.* SHIVERS *and the* CANON *laugh.*)

CANON

That means a row with Father Shaughnessy.

SHIVERS

There'll be a row with him whether or no. (*Pause*) Canon, this affair of his can't go on.

CANON

(*Uneasily*)

For God's sake, go easy now, Michael.

SHIVERS

How can you go easy with this sort of thing? It is a downright liberty, and his bullyin' and dragoonin' and refusin' to baptise the mixed marriage children are liberties, too. We are not being kicked down the lanes of the eighteenth and nineteenth centuries now, Canon.

CANON

(*Dismally*)

Sure, I'm always tellin' him. It's all routine now, and no faith. As if it was anything but faith that dragged us all out of the pit.

SHIVERS

Well, I'm tellin' you straight, Canon—that's why I'm here. I'm takin' my stand on my rights as a citizen and the majority of the people down there are quietly doing the same. Do you know what I mean, Canon?

CANON

I know it's never the right of anyone to do the wrong thing. You should keep away from Nora Fintry, Michael; she's not for *you*.

SHIVERS

Did I ever say she was? I don't care two straws for the girshe. I just get seen with her to uphold a principle; call it spite if you like.

CANON

That's a terrible admission to make.

SHIVERS

That's human nature, and right well you know it, Canon.

CANON

(*Pensively*)

So it is . . . I'm a spiteful oul' divil meself with Rosieanne. (ROSIEANNE *knocks and enters excitedly.*)

ROSIEANNE

Canon, the child is here now with the mother to be baptised. Are you able?

CANON

I am, in the name of God.

SHIVERS

So, *you* are doin' a bit of sedition too, are you? Baptisin' a child behind his back.

CANON

There's no use, Michael, in sittin' tryin' to keep the world from turning. Here, Rosieanne, help me in and stand sponsor for the child. Did you bring in a drop of holy water from the font?

ROSIEANNE

It's all ready, Canon.

SHIVERS

Good luck, Canon. Common sense is surely the white black-bird nowadays. (*He goes first.* ROSIEANNE *wheels the* CANON *towards the door.*)

CANON

(*As they go*)

Did the Widow mention about the butter, Rosieanne?

ROSIEANNE

Sure, wait till you see the kitchen table with butter—as much as would feed a regiment.

CANON

(*In ecstasy*)

Glory be to God! (*Before they reach the door it opens and* FATHER SHAUGHNESSY, *carrying a sheaf of papers, comes in angrily.*)

FATHER SHAUGHNESSY

What is going on here? What does that man Shivers want?
What is this child doing crying in the hall here? Speak,
woman!

ROSIEANNE

(*Fearfully*)

It's—it's the Widow Whelan's grandchild, Father, that's to
be baptised.

FATHER SHAUGHNESSY

Didn't I definitely refuse this rebellious and disobedient
woman?

CANON

Maybe you did, but me foot's down and I'm goin' to do
it meself.

FATHER SHAUGHNESSY

You certainly are not. I forbid it. You are retired.

CANON

(*Ragingly*)

I'm not retired.

FATHER SHAUGHNESSY

Well, you are disabled and I am in charge here. I will not
allow you to counter my order, Canon! Let me tell you I
have seen the Bishop this morning and we have arranged
definitely for your removal to a quiet home in Dalkey.

CANON

What's that! Damn the foot I'll move.

FATHER SHAUGHNESSY

You'll not have to. The Bishop's car and his personal servant will be here presently to take you away.

121

CANON

Very well! But you'll need at least another dozen along with yourself to shift *me* out of here. I'm in with the bricks an' I'm stayin' till they fall down.

FATHER SHAUGHNESSY

We'll see! And this woman and her child are getting out of here. (*He stamps out in a temper, closing the door behind him. The* CANON *and* ROSIEANNE *wait tensely listening. There is an altercation outside and the noise of a heavy door closing.*)

CANON

(*As the door closes*)

We're beat, Rosieanne. If only the Blessed Mother would let me walk. . . . Wheel me in, Rosieanne, to the little altar, till I tell her the wretch and the villain that I am.

ROSIEANNE

(*Sympathetically*)

Sure, she knows and knows, Canon. (FATHER SHAUGHNESSY *enters and crosses.*)

FATHER SHAUGHNESSY

Rose, you will send Meg to me instantly.

ROSIEANNE

I will, Father.

CANON

Meg's gone, if it's any news to you.

FATHER SHAUGHNESSY

Gone! What's this? Who sent her away?

122

CANON

Who but yourself. She's gone to work with Shivers, a decent man who won't throw the poor girl's tarts out of the window. Wheel me out of this, Rosieanne. (*They pass out quietly.* FATHER SHAUGHNESSY *walks up and down with grim features. The minutes pass. Noise of a car approaching and stopping is heard.* FATHER SHAUGHNESSY *looks out of the window.* ROSIEANNE *knocks and enters.*)

ROSIEANNE

If you please, Father, the Bishop's car is here and his man is inquiring for the Canon.

FATHER SHAUGHNESSY

Then have Canon Lavelle carefully wrapped for the journey. His belongings can be sent after him.

ROSIEANNE

But he won't budge, Father.

FATHER SHAUGHNESSY

You have your orders, Rose.

ROSIEANNE

But the Canon's locked himself in the Oratory, chair and all, and he won't come out.

FATHER SHAUGHNESSY
(*Irascibly*)

This is ludicrous. He must come out. I insist on his coming out. Go, give the Bishop's man some tea in the kitchen, and I'll have things arranged by that.

123

ROSIEANNE

Very well, Father. (*She turns at the door*) Mr. Dillon's here, Father Shaughnessy, an' he's very funny-looking.

FATHER SHAUGHNESSY
(*Irascibly*)

Did you ever see him when he wasn't funny-looking? Send him in at once. (*She nods and goes. A moment later,* DENIS DILLON *comes in. He is flushed and his eyes are dilated. He takes off his hat unsteadily, hiccoughs and stares at* FATHER SHAUGHNESSY. *Regarding him closely*) Well, Mr. Dillon, what seems to be the matter with you?

DILLON
(*Unsteadily*)

The times are out of joint, Father Shaughnessy.

FATHER SHAUGHNESSY
(*Regarding him more closely*)

I am not in any mood for facetiousness, Mr. Dillon. Have you performed the duties I assigned to you today?

DILLON
(*Smoothly*)

I have, Father, as I always do and as my kind have always done. I took your bag of coppers and instead of going out and buyin' a Potter's field like the Judas I felt myself, I went to Shivers's pub, planked it down on the counter and drank every penny of it. Then I went to the station for your *Catholic Firesides* and your *Dundooley Sentinels* and what-the-hell-nots, and I made them run races with one another all over the windy roads. (*Pause*) And here I am.

FATHER SHAUGHNESSY

(*Holding himself in*)

You have been drinking!

DILLON

I have. I and Judas Iscariot drowned our remorse together.

FATHER SHAUGHNESSY

In the strict interests of morality, I summarily suspend you meantime from the school.

DILLON

(*Maudlinly*)

It is not new to me to be suspended, Father Shaughnessy. All my life I have been suspended by a piece of whip-gut over the edge of a precipice and all about me dark saints frown and jabber in my ears and away below me, little black priests read their breviaries and see in me the justice of God.

FATHER SHAUGHNESSY

(*Grimly*)

This is disgusting before me. (*Imperatively*) Sober yourself, fellow, in my presence.

DILLON

To be sober is to be afraid again—afraid of your black cloth and your eyes and your collar.

FATHER SHAUGHNESSY

(*Suddenly striking him with the back of his hand across the face*)

Will that sober you?

DILLON

(*Wincing and stung. After a pause*)

A little, perhaps. Sufficient for me to recognize another Irish clerical privilege.

FATHER SHAUGHNESSY

You are insolent, incredibly insolent. Get out of here and report to me when you are sober. Then I will deal with you.

DILLON

(*Turning slowly*)

When I'm sober . . . when the mountains fall upon me. (*Sudden noise of cheering and shouting without.* ROSIEANNE *enters excitedly.*)

ROSIEANNE

Father, Patrick Hearty is dragging the girl Nora Fintry up the street. They're coming in here.

FATHER SHAUGHNESSY

(*Calmly*)

Then admit them instantly and without concern.

ROSIEANNE

But there's a whole crowd of people followin' them, cheerin' and shoutin' at them.

FATHER SHAUGHNESSY

Take no notice of them. Admit only my officer and his prisoner. (*She nods and goes.* DILLON *turns a little drunkenly and stares at the priest.*)

DILLON

Prisoner! A strange word that! Nora will never be anyone's prisoner.

126

FATHER SHAUGHNESSY

I will deal with this insolence at another time, Dillon. (*Loud knocks on the door, right. It is flung open and* PATRICK HEARTY *drags in* NORA FINTRY *and throws her forward. He looks exhausted and is panting.* NORA *is dishevelled, her clothes are torn and her hair tossed about her face. From outside comes the noise of talking and discussion and arguing during the rest of this scene.*)

HEARTY

Your orders, Father Shaughnessy.

FATHER SHAUGHNESSY

So be it. I will answer for it.

HEARTY
(*Pointing to* DILLON)

And that man, Father, refused to help us in any way. He's a traitor.

FATHER SHAUGHNESSY

For this, Denis Dillon, you are summarily dismissed from the school.

DILLON
(*Shakingly*)

We begin to ascend. Hold on to me, Nora, for I am not used to ascending.

NORA

I am closer to you now, Denis, than I have ever been to you before, or to anyone.

HEARTY
(*Irascibly*)

Now we're going to have the meek martyrs dyin' together. I'd have none of that, Father.

NORA

You'll find nothing very meek about me, Brigadier General Hearty. You may think yourself a lion panting after virtue, but you're just an old miley cow to me. (DILLON *laughs hilariously. Cries come from outside, cries of "Leave the girshe alone." "Come out, Hearty, and fight with men."*)

HEARTY

(*Squaring up to* DILLON)

I will put your yellow teeth down your neck, schoolmaster!

FATHER SHAUGHNESSY

(*Calmly*)

On the contrary, Mr. Hearty, you will stand erect in your position, and preserve your dignity as a moral policeman.

HEARTY

But this is unbearable provocation, Father!

FATHER SHAUGHNESSY

Provocation is the acid test of character. Return to your former position and make a report.

HEARTY

(*Saluting and crossing*)

This evening, Father, when in the company of Officers Driscoll, Martin, Nolan and O'Brien and Woman Officer Brodigan, we saw the man Shivers and the girl Nora Fintry, openly and brazenly associating in a motor car. I immediately searched for the secretary, Denis Dillon.

FATHER SHAUGHNESSY

Where did you find him?

128

HEARTY

I found him in Shivers's public house.

FATHER SHAUGHNESSY

Describe his exact position.

HEARTY

He had piles of pennies all round him and he was building a castle with them, drinkin' Scotch and soda and singin' a disgraceful ballad. I asked him to co-operate with me.

FATHER SHAUGHNESSY

What was his answer?

HEARTY

He pointed at me and called me a Firbolg.

FATHER SHAUGHNESSY

A what?

HEARTY

A Firbolg.

FATHER SHAUGHNESSY

What's that?

HEARTY

One of them little black men, Father, that you see in Joyce's History, Part I. (DILLON *and* NORA *laugh. Cries come from outside, cries of "Speech. Speech. Leave the lassie alone. Come outside and fight."*)

FATHER SHAUGHNESSY
(*Softly*)

What did you do?

HEARTY

I threw him against the counter as one unworthy of his position and returned to my men.

FATHER SHAUGHNESSY

(*Calmly*)

You had no right whatever, as a moral policeman, to throw him against the counter. Proceed.

HEARTY

I decided with the help of Officer Brigid Brodigan to seize Nora Fintry and take her before you here.

FATHER SHAUGHNESSY

What was her attitude?

HEARTY

She scratched and kicked and shouted and her language was ungodly. Brigid Brodigan is now getting a patch on her face at the chemist's.

FATHER SHAUGHNESSY

And the man, Michael Shivers.

HEARTY

I detailed Officers Driscoll, Martin, Nolan and O'Brien to arrest him.

FATHER SHAUGHNESSY

To your knowledge, did he resist arrest?

HEARTY

He did, Father. They're still battlin' below on the bridge.

FATHER SHAUGHNESSY

Why didn't you call on the people for assistance?

HEARTY

The people round at the time were agin us. It's the free drinks Shivers gives them, Father.

FATHER SHAUGHNESSY

Is there evidence to support that?

HEARTY

I think we could get sworn evidence.

FATHER SHAUGHNESSY

Then that hotel must be placed out of bounds to our Catholic parishioners. (*Pause*) What of the Civil Police?

HEARTY

The Inspector and his men stood lookin' on.

DILLON

So was *I* lookin' on from Shivers's doorway, don't forget that.

NORA

And when I get out of here, I'll not stand looking on either.

FATHER SHAUGHNESSY
(*Calmly*)

A deplorable attitude, child. Will you please be silent and allow me to deal as gently as possible with you.

DILLON

Lift the crumb from the table of your master, Nora.

NORA

(*Breaking out violently*)

No man is my master. No damned generation of clerics will hunt *me* down. I am a daughter of what was here before you all and a mother of what will be here after you are all gone.

FATHER SHAUGHNESSY

(*Quietly*)

You are tiring yourself out unnecessarily, child. I think we can allow you to sit. Bring a chair, Patrick Hearty.

HEARTY

(*Sullenly*)

Not me. She's called me out of my name.

FATHER SHAUGHNESSY

You will carry out my instructions instantly. (HEARTY *immediately places the chair beside* NORA) You may sit.

NORA

I refuse.

FATHER SHAUGHNESSY

I ask you to sit.

NORA

(*Suddenly heaving the chair across the room*)

And that is my answer. (*Dead silence follows.* HEARTY *strikes a threatening attitude.*)

HEARTY

I wouldn't tolerate that, Father.

FATHER SHAUGHNESSY
(*Calmly*)

Can I not teach you patience? Can I not make you remember whose work you are doing? As an example to this poor undisciplined girl and to you also, I myself will retrieve the chair. (*He crosses, lifts the fallen chair and places it in its former position. As he places the chair*) And now, we shall proceed. (*Enter* ROSIEANNE *perturbed.*)

ROSIEANNE

Please, Father, the Bishop's man is finished his tea and he says he can't wait all night.

FATHER SHAUGHNESSY

Where is Canon Lavelle?

ROSIEANNE

Sure, he's still in the Oratory, Father, and he won't come out.

FATHER SHAUGHNESSY

This is unspeakable. See that he gets no food until he returns to his room and instruct the Bishop's servant to remain meanwhile.

ROSIEANNE

Very well, Father, and there's a crowd of people wantin' in.

FATHER SHAUGHNESSY

Let nobody in. (*Cries and shouting outside.*)

ROSIEANNE

Nora Fintry's father is standing crying at the door.

FATHER SHAUGHNESSY

You may allow him in, Rosieanne, in case we are in the least unfair. (ROSIEANNE *nods and goes off.*)

DILLON

Standin' cryin' at the priest's door. There's somethin' that echoes far back in that.

FATHER SHAUGHNESSY

For that malicious remark, Denis Dillon, you are placed under arrest as an enemy of the Vigilance Committee. (HEARTY *moves up beside* DILLON.)

DILLON

What does it matter? I have been under arrest since I was born. I have been inside the netting wire that runs round the clerical gardens.

HEARTY

Enough of that cheek or I'll quieten you.

NORA

Keep your heart up, Denis. They can take our bread and butter, but they can't take what we had before they came to the land at all. (*Enter* PHELIM FINTRY *distressed. He looks about him worried and downcast.*)

PHELIM

(*Pathetically to* NORA)

There! What did I tell you! I could see this before me like a dog on the road. Enemies—always makin' enemies, didn't I say?—

NORA

Stop whining, father, and take me home out of this place.

134

PHELIM

How can I take you home, and all hands here agin you?

DILLON

I will take you home, Nora.

HEARTY

(*Grimly*)

Aye, schoolmaster, when the priest says it.

DILLON

If only I was able, Nora.

NORA

You are able in the heart, Denis, never mind. (DILLON *hangs his head.*)

FATHER SHAUGHNESSY

Each of you must first openly express sorrow before me for having publicly outraged the moral law, and for the grave scandal you have given, and you must both give an assurance to live a fit and proper life in the future and to co-operate in the spirit and in the letter with my Vigilance Committee.

NORA

(*Flashing out*)

I was not born to give you, or any of you, assurances.

DILLON

And that answer will do for me, too. (*Pause.*)

FATHER SHAUGHNESSY

(*Grimly, after the pause*)

Nora Fintry, are you going to exhaust my patience with you?

NORA

What's your patience to me, Father Shaughnessy? You're just to me a man I rub shoulders with in a dark street, and forget.

PHELIM

For God's sake, Nora, don't anger the priest. You'll not be the better of it the morrow or the day after. Can't you say the word that he wants you to say? What's there in a word?

NORA

There's always been one in Ireland who thought the whole of life was in a word. I was born of such a one.

PHELIM

You were born of *me,* Nora, an' I didn't learn you that.

NORA

It's your old double bed you're thinking of, father. Only for that you'd swear you never saw me before.

DILLON

That's it. The double beds and the clerical gardens—the twin jailors that deny us life.

HEARTY

How far are we to put with this, Father?

FATHER SHAUGHNESSY

Do you two want to provoke me to the use of sterner measures? You are both a menace in my parish. You will either repent of your misdeeds and give suitable assurances or leave my parish.

NORA

I will give you nothing, and I will remain in my own home, where I belong.

DILLON

An' I will dig myself in beside you, Nora.

FATHER SHAUGHNESSY

(*In passion*)

Stand forward, Phelim Fintry.

PHELIM

(*Shakingly*)

Yes—yes, Father. Sure, I will do anything I—I can, Father.

FATHER SHAUGHNESSY

You will refuse this girl your house until she consents to give us the promises we require of her.

PHELIM

It's—it's hard, Father. But if you say it.

FATHER SHAUGHNESSY

I have said it. (PHELIM *bows his head*) And that is only a beginning. I will leave this woman so that not even the dogs on the street will recognize her.

PHELIM

(*Crossing*)

I suppose I may go home now, to my empty house and stay there. Who wants a man with a daughter that the priest's agin? (*He goes forlornly.*)

DILLON

(*Pointing after* PHELIM)

There we are, all of us, since the wild geese flew screaming away. We wear coercion like an inside shirt.

HEARTY

(*Striking* DILLON)

That's enough out of you.

DILLON

Keep your hands off me, you Firbolg, you priest's police-man. (*Violent knocking without and cries.* INSPECTOR TOOMEY *tired and dishevelled enters dramatically, right, and surveys the room. There is a deep pause.*)

FATHER SHAUGHNESSY

(*After the pause*)

What is your business, Inspector Toomey?

TOOMEY

I have just arrested the four men, Driscoll, Martin, Nolan and O'Brien and I now arrest you, Patrick Hearty, for assault and battery and doing grievous bodily harm to Nora Fintry and Michael Shivers. (*He takes hold of him.*)

FATHER SHAUGHNESSY

This is an outrage. These moral officers acted expressly on my orders.

TOOMEY

(*With spirit*)

Am I to take it then, Father Shaughnessy, that you aided and abetted these people in a breach of the civil law?

FATHER SHAUGHNESSY

(*Impatiently*)

I want none of your police jargon. Put it that way if you like.

TOOMEY

(*Angrily*)

Your admission leaves me with no alternative. I warned you before I never count the cost of doing my duty clean or dirty. I'll probably pay for this but I'm doing it all the same. (*Pause*) As an officer of the law, I arrest you, Father Shaughnessy, and charge you with being a menace to the public peace and with inciting people to acts of criminal violence in defiance of the civil law.

HEARTY

(*Violently asserting himself*)

You stupid bobby! You can't arrest the priest. Lay one hand on him and b · the Lord . . .

FATHER SHAUGHNESSY

One moment, Patrick Hearty. You will allow him to do his duty as he sees it. (*Pause*) Proceed, Toomey.

TOOMEY

I'll do it whether he stops me or not. I'd brain him where he stands. You will accompany me to the police station. No doubt bail can be arranged there.

FATHER SHAUGHNESSY

I am quite ready.

HEARTY

Not a bit of it. (*He runs excitedly to the window back and starts shouting*) Hey, men and women out there, do yous know that the priest is arrested? Are yous going to see hand-cuffs on the priest? (*Cries of horror and menacing shouts.*)

VOICES

Who's touchin' the priest? Who's arrestin' the priest?

HEARTY

(*Shouting at the window*)

Are yous goin' to let the priest be took to the barracks? (*More cries and shouting.*)

FATHER SHAUGHNESSY

(*To* TOOMEY)

Are you quite sure, policeman, that my people are against me?

TOOMEY

It matters nothing to me who the people are with. I'll do my duty if Hell opens.

VOICES

Let us in. We want that bloody bobby. Let him touch the priest if he dares. We'll kick the bobby down the road.

HEARTY

Now we'll see.

TOOMEY

Aye, we'll see. This is not the first dirty job I've had to carry through, and it won't be the last! If I fail, then there's no law in this land except the priest's law.

DILLON

(*With a laugh*)

The Inspector has made a discovery. Give him a medal.

TOOMEY

Shut up, Dillon, or I'll arrest you too.

DILLON

You can't arrest a man that's already arrested. I'm a prisoner of the Holy Office.

FATHER SHAUGHNESSY

I am ready waiting to accompany you to the Barracks, Inspector Toomey.

TOOMEY

(*Firmly*)

And so you will. (*He crosses purposefully to the window*) Men and women of this town. I warn you all that any interference with me in the execution of my duty will mean scores of arrests and trials for lawlessness. I advise you to disperse to your homes at once for I'll shoot my way through you if I must. (*A shower of cries and shouts.*)

VOICES

Leave the priest alone! You dare touch the priest, you bloody bobby! (*A shower of stones smashes against the window.* TOOMEY *falls back.*)

FATHER SHAUGHNESSY

Did you say—shoot your way?

TOOMEY

That's what I said—and it won't be the first time.

VOICES

Let us in! Let us in! We want the bobby.

FATHER SHAUGHNESSY

(*Going to the window*)

My people, I want you to face this crisis calmly and with Christian dignity. You are now, as always, the custodians of the moral name and fame of our country, treasures which we store eternally in our souls. Don't be distressed, it is not the first time that one of your priests has gone to a prison cell. . . .

DILLON

The new Mark Anthony! You damn fool, Toomey. Have you no brains?

TOOMEY

(*Prohibiting further speech*)

I will not allow this incitement. Stand back. (FATHER SHAUGHNESSY *returns from the window.* NORA *watches him closely.*)

NORA

(*Bitterly*)

That was the act of a cruel man—not of a priest.

FATHER SHAUGHNESSY

So I have disappointed our pagan heroine, have I? How much would I disappoint you, if in justice I sent you and Dillon out of here and told my people you were my enemies?

TOOMEY

I would prevent that. They both have the secular independence I shot men down for and hid in haystacks for, and blew lorries of British soldiers sky-high for. And priest or no priest you'll not snatch it from them.

NORA

Thank you, Inspector. That's the first time that's been said in Irish history.

TOOMEY

Don't thank me, lassie. It's my job and I hate the damn thing like poison. But I'll do it all the same. That's the soldier's make-up.

HEARTY

(*To the* INSPECTOR)

Are you daft enough to think that the people are goin' to let you get away with arrestin' the priest?

TOOMEY

(*Determined*)

I will not be intimidated. (*Angrily*) You will be handcuffed together and I will clear a way with these. (*He takes out his baton and a gun*) Get ready to leave, all.

FATHER SHAUGHNESSY

(*Grimly*)

We are ready. You are free to take us, policeman—at your peril.

TOOMEY

At my peril then! And so be it. Come along. (*The door is suddenly flung open, left, and* ROSIEANNE *runs in.*)

ROSIEANNE

(*Waving her hands*)

The Canon! Father, the Canon! (*She runs back again. All turn and stare at the door. A moment later* CANON LAVELLE *appears and walks with fair steps and with the aid of a stick into the room. He is greeted with a shower of ejaculations.*)

143

ALL TOGETHER

Canon!

FATHER SHAUGHNESSY
(*Staring at him*)

This—is incredible.

CANON
(*Crossing to* FATHER SHAUGHNESSY)

Faith is always incredible, Father Shaughnessy, to the mathematician. (*Cries of shouting and cursing without*) What is still more incredible is that your blundering has made raving wolves out of my harmless sheep. Listen to that!

FATHER SHAUGHNESSY
(*Stopping the Canon as he moves towards the window*)

You can't interfere in this. I forbid it. You must await the Bishop's ruling.

CANON

I will do as I think fit. There are lives at stake. (*A tense pause as they regard each other.*)

FATHER SHAUGHNESSY
(*In a temper*)

Very well, I have warned you. I withdraw as a protest. (*He slams the table angrily and sits down.*)

VOICES

The Canon! The Canon! Hurrah for the Canon!

CANON
(*At the window, hammering with his stick sharply*)

I'll hurrah yous if I come out, the—the damned cheek of you all. Is that you I see there, Christy Lamb, and the poor cows below waitin' to be milked? And you, Sarah Pender,

who's mindin' your children and you there like a brazen fag-
got? An' Peadar Coyne. I'll go down, Peadar, and raise you
on me toe with a kick, so I will. An' you, Nancy Ryan, I never
saw you with a clean house in my life an' there you are, an'
you, Phil Brady, that put the heel on my boot that came off
in a week. A grand cobbler you are, standin' there, ravin' and
shoutin', an' of course we wouldn't be right without you, Bar-
ney Comiskey. How did you manage to drag your elbow off
the counter to come up and see me? An' you, you lazy imp,
Aggie Slaven, an' the ashes meetin' me at the door whenever
I go to your house. A fine set yous all are, makin' a public
show an' laugh of my parish, an' the man from the *Independent* sittin' there on the wall writin' it all down and
burstin' with the laughin'. Get home out of that this minute,
to your work an' your children an' when I say Mass the morrow I will not have me tongue in me cheek when I'm talkin'
to you. (*Noise of people moving away and then silence. The*
CANON *slams the window tight, then crosses and confronts the
others.*)

CANON
(*Tapping with his stick*)
Patrick Hearty, when I was strong on me props, did I or
did I not lead you home often of a night, when you had more
drink in you than would stupefy a donkey?

HEARTY
You maybe did, Canon.

CANON
There's no maybe about it at all.

HEARTY
That's all over now, Canon.

CANON

I see. You're a drunkard no longer. You have changed all that to be a common hooligan, defyin' the law and assaultin' your neighbors.

HEARTY

I done it on the priest's orders.

CANON

You did it for your own glorification. Knocking the daylights out of your neighbors for the greater honor and glory of God is a worse disease than leprosy. Go home to your big ass of a wife an' I'll see if I can coax the Inspector here not to land you below in the jail.

HEARTY

All right, Canon, if you want me to go, I'll go. There's a devil the size of an elephant in that fellow Toomey, and I want nothin' to do with him. (*He crosses.*)

TOOMEY

You're right, Hearty. I'd think as much of braining you as I would of strangling a weasel. (HEARTY *goes, a little surlily. The* CANON *looks sympathetically at* NORA, *who is now pale and exhausted.*)

CANON

Nora, you look as if you were dragged out of a shuck. Take her in, Dillon, and get Rosieanne to give her a cup of hot tea.

DILLON

I will, Canon. Come on, Nora. (NORA *listlessly allows* DILLON *to take her off, left. The* CANON *watches her go, then turns to* TOOMEY *with a shake of his head.*)

146

CANON

(*Eyeing* TOOMEY)

Well, Inspector, may I congratulate you? You're the grandest and the greatest idiot in all Ireland. You have actually arrested a priest for breaking the law.

TOOMEY

And why not, Canon? I've killed men out of a sense of duty and I consider myself an honest man.

CANON

Honest men, Toomey, can sometimes be damned nuisances. That's why the Greeks killed Socrates, and quite right too. Did you ever hear of the law of come and go, of the law of Nelson and his blind eye? When the English, who have the wisdom of all mediocre people, are menaced by Communism, they don't shoot them down, do they? They picture them in comic papers with beards and bombs and laugh them out of existence. We, who are more learned but less wise, should do likewise with our Holy Willies on the one hand like Hearty and his Vigilance men, and our pagans on the other hand like Dillon and our little firebrand Nora.

TOOMEY

I'm no philosopher, Canon. Philosophy to me is a juggling with words to evade an honest issue. As a man under orders, I do what I must do and no bones about it. Can you give me a guarantee this is all over?

CANON

I can, and you can depend on me word, as a strictly dishonest old rascal.

TOOMEY

Good enough, Canon. God save what's left of happiness from honest fanatics like me and that priest over there. (*The* INSPECTOR *goes.* FATHER SHAUGHNESSY, *who has been sitting silently looking fixedly before him, now rises slowly and confronts the* CANON.)

FATHER SHAUGHNESSY

Canon Lavelle! I have remained silent all this time so as not to cause a brawl. I may tell you straight I am not going to take this high-handed presumption of yours lying down.

CANON

Neither am I going to allow you to make my parish the cockpit of your theories.

FATHER SHAUGHNESSY

Your blundering and old-fashioned heroics have ruined everything I have achieved.

CANON

What have you achieved? You have only succeeded in stupidly dragging into the light the things we old codgers grow in the dark in Ireland.

FATHER SHAUGHNESSY

I will allow nothing to grow in the dark in the new Ireland we are building.

CANON

Of course you won't, because you're a hot-headed pioneer full of spiritual snobbery. Ten thousand sages of the Church have refused to write certain laws on paper, but you rushing in with a Gaelic tag in your mouth, scrawl them across a page with a schoolboy's pen. Let me tell you this, that we rule this nation with laws that no one writes but that everyone instinctively accepts. You can cross out a law that's on paper, but you can't cross out a law that has never been written. The day you put these laws on paper in this country, you and I and all we stand for will have to take the field and fight to the death for our continuance. You think I'm an oul' fool, because I speak to my people in their own language, but instead I am what Christ cautioned us to be, as simple as a dove, but as wise as a serpent.

FATHER SHAUGHNESSY
(Angrily)
I believe none of these things you say—not a syllable. They're theologically crooked and dishonest.

CANON
You'll believe one day in cold steel in your stomach, an' that's the answer to your damned moral gymnastics. And there's more Toomeys and more men of blood and duty in this country than your idiocy can see. (ROSIEANNE *enters.*)

ROSIEANNE
Please, Canon, what am I to do with the Bishop's man? He's stamping up and down, callin' me names and he wants more tea because the schoolmaster and Nora are gettin' some.

CANON
Tell him to take this letter I have written direct to the Bishop. (*Hands her a letter.*)

FATHER SHAUGHNESSY
Wait. (*A pause*) Tell him, Rose, to prepare instantly to drive me to the Bishop's residence.

ROSIEANNE

Yes, Father! (*She goes, carrying the* CANON'*s letter.*)

FATHER SHAUGHNESSY

We shall argue no further. This is a matter for the Bishop.

CANON

Go ahead, an' if his Right Reverence is half as shrewd as I think he is, he'll send you to Glasgow where Communists are two a penny and Holy Willies are nineteen to the dozen.

FATHER SHAUGHNESSY
(*Irascibly*)

Pah! I have been too fair with you. It is one of my weaknesses with people. (*He stamps out. The* CANON *looks strangely after him.* ROSIEANNE *enters.*)

ROSIEANNE

Are you sure you're all right, Canon? For God's sake, sit down an' don't overdo it all at once.

CANON

I will, Rosieanne. (*She places a chair for him and he sits.*)

ROSIEANNE

It was the Mother of God herself that done it, Canon, an' that mob round the door an' the Inspector's blood up and the skin and hair ready for the flyin'.

CANON

Yes, it was that, Rosieanne. I prayed and prayed in the dark like the way our poor fathers must have done long ago on the dark sides of the mountains and I felt as if they were crowdin' round me an' the mud of the black years on their cheeks. (*Pause. He looks at* ROSIEANNE) Let you not be sayin' a word of this to anyone with your clatterin' tongue.

ROSIEANNE

I won't breathe it, Canon. (*Enter left,* NORA *and* DILLON.)

CANON

Well, did you two have something to eat?

DILLON

We had hot tea and we needed it, Canon.

CANON

Aye. Well, it's time I had some too. Go on, Rosieanne, an' see about it. An' you might send a message down to the Widow Whelan an' the others that have the unbaptised children to bring all the babies up to me in the mornin' till I christen them.

DILLON

I'll run down and tell her myself, Canon. It's only a hen's race and *she'll* tell the others. (ROSIEANNE *nods and goes out, left.*)

CANON

Go ahead then, Denis, if you are anxious to be a law-abiding citizen again. (*The* CANON *grins and* DILLON *laughs.*)

DILLON

Don't forget, I'm an ex-schoolmaster, Canon.

CANON

Och, ex your grannie. You will go to the school on Monday morning, as usual.

DILLON
(*At the door, turning*)
Do you mean, Canon, that I'm not dismissed?

CANON
Don't be an ass, Dillon. (*Pause*) And I like my teachers to be married. It settles them down.

DILLON
(*Appealingly*)
Nora, do you think if I went back to the school . . . (*He stops and looks at her.*)

NORA
(*Vehemently*)
So, you want to go on being a message boy and the Canon's parish clerk. Is that what it all comes to?

CANON
Now, what kind of talk is that, Nora?

NORA
He must choose. This is one of the things must be said, Canon. You want him to run your messages and be your parish clerk. I want him to go out and meet life and not hide from it, to cease being a servant, and to begin being the giant that every man should build up within himself, yes, to charge windmills, if need be, to believe with me that no law is stronger than life. For these I want him, Canon, and I won't share.

DILLON
Then, neither will I share, Nora. (*Pause*) Canon, I refuse your offer of the school.

CANON

(*Going to* DILLON)

It's easy, Dillon, to be heroic when the blood runs hot. But how hot is the blood when your wife is hungry and with child and the fire won't light because there's no coal?

DILLON

(*Aghast*)

God, don't say that to me, Canon.

CANON

Aye, I'll say it to you. It's another of the things must be said.

DILLON

I . . . I . . . I couldn't bear that. . . . It's all so uncertain. If I went back to the school for security, would you not try and see a little of the way with me?

NORA

(*Slowly*)

You asked me, Denis, to lift you up and set you free. I've tried and failed. Good-bye, Canon. I'm going away.

CANON

Now you're being silly and stupid, Nora. You're not going back to England, I hope.

NORA

No, I will never leave Ireland again. There's something here that is nowhere else. It's away back far and away deep down. A man going down a moonlit road from a fair may know it, or a child reading on a broken window sill of Niam or Aideen or Maeve, but they will tell you no name for it. They will look away from you and the tears will come with a sudden wild rush, but the cry is within them forever, and neither money nor mating will make them happy. (*Pause*) I am like that, Canon. It's my only sin, and this is my only true confession. Do you know now, why I could not say the wretched word for poor Father Shaughnessy . . . or why I can't be the wife of your parish clerk? (*Pause. She looks at the* CANON *with suffering eyes and goes to the door.*)

DILLON

Have pity on me, Nora.

NORA

I have no pity, Denis, for a man who wants to live on in servitude. I have been born out of warriors, poets, saints and heroes; and am I to bear children to a servant?

DILLON

But there's no way, Nora. Can't he see there's no way?

NORA

When there's no way, what do all great people and nations do? They blaze a way. But cowards sit in the mud and complain against God. There's my father's land that needs working and the field at the back needs draining and tilled. There's the growing of things in the earth—the joy of seeing them flower, and there's *me*. I will have a free man or no man. (*She pushes him away*) Out of my way, Denis, a shrewd old man sets a penny mousetrap for you and you blunder into it. I will find what I am seeking without you. (*She goes off with pride and hauteur.* DILLON *turns from the door to the* CANON. *They look at each other.*)

154

DILLON

(*Brokenly*)

I . . . I will go now, Canon. . . . I will report for duty on Monday morning.

CANON

(*As in a dream*)

So you will . . . and be sure not to be late, for there's piles of parish work for you that's been neglected.

DILLON

Very well, Canon, good night. (*He goes, back.*)

CANON

(*Slowly*)

Good night.

DILLON

(*Turning at the door with sudden spirit*)

Canon, if—if you were me, what would *you* do?

CANON

(*Acidly*)

Go home, Dillon. I'm not you.

DILLON

(*Flashing in*)

You'd throw the school to hell, and go out after her. You'd drain Phelim's fields for her and dig in them till your back would break and you'd laugh through it all, wouldn't you? Go on, Canon, tell me! Tell me the truth!

CANON

I'll tell you nothing.

155

DILLON

You're afraid—afraid I'll find out the truth of it all.

CANON

Damnation to your cheek, Dillon.

DILLON

And damnation to your slavery. To hell with your school. I'm going out to find Nora and I'll drain and dig and plant for her till my body aches. And Nora and I will fight you to the last.

CANON

(*Looking at him, after a long pause*)

Now, you're a man, Dillon, and there won't be any fighting to be done. I am afraid neither of Nora nor of her children-to-be. And a wiser and finer Ireland needn't be afraid of them either. I am toppling to the grave, but that is my faith. I may be wrong but I don't think somehow that I am. Now go, Denis, and even if she wants you up on a pagan steed, get right beside her. It will not take you astray—her white steed has not come down the centuries for nothing.

DILLON

I will, Canon. And forgive me for bursting out against you.

CANON

Och, your grannie. Stop asking people to forgive you and begin telling them to go to blazes. (DILLON *goes off in bright spirits. The* CANON *turns weakly, staggers a little and blunders to a chair, into which he settles himself pensively. He lifts his eyes slowly to the picture of the Blessed Virgin.*)

THE WHITE STEED

CANON

(To the picture, with conversational intimacy)

Well, Holy Mother, we're used to these little mountain storms, but, sure, the mountains remain. So we needn't be afraid, need we now?

(The Curtain Falls Slowly)

COGGERERS

"A terrible beauty now is born . . ."
W. B. YEATS

TO

PEARL

WHO MADE ME SIT DOWN AND FINISH IT

CHARACTERS

Brigid Anne Galgoogley, *an old charwoman*

Oweneen, *her son about nineteen*

Eamonn O'Curry, *a librarian*

Statues of John Mitchell, Lord Edward Fitzgerald, Wolf Tone, Robert Emmet and Charles Stewart Parnell

———

The action passes in the entrance hall of a Dublin City Library, during the morning of Easter Monday, 1916.

———

This play was first produced at the Abbey Theatre, Dublin, in November, 1934, under the direction of Hugh Hunt, with settings by Tanya Moiseiwitsch.

SCENE

The Entrance Hall of a Dublin City Library in the vicinity of St. Stephen's Green. From left to right are five pedestals surmounted by busts of MITCHELL, LORD EDWARD FITZGERALD, TONE, EMMET *and* PARNELL.

To the back, right, is a low white slab, made as a base for a reclining figure. It is now empty, its figure having been removed for repair. The names of the patriots are conspicuously inscribed on their respective pedestals. The empty slab bears the inscription "DAN O'CONNELL."

A door, back, center, to the library shelves, and a door, right, leading outside.

It is early morning on Easter Monday, 1916.

As the curtain rises, the stage is half-lit and misty. There is deep silence. Then comes a ship's siren call from the Liffey, then the voice of a newsboy in the distance, Indepen'ent *and* Irish Times, *then the sudden chirruping of birds from St. Stephen's Green. A clock strikes rhythmically somewhere. The door, back, center, opens and* EAMONN O'CURRY, *a dark, middle-aged man, comes in, hatless and with pen and papers in his hand. He looks round him. He is nervous.*

O'CURRY

Is there anyone there? (*He crosses to the door, right, and looks out, then returns to the statues*) If yous only knew! . . . (*He looks about him again nervously and goes off, back.* MRS. GALGOOGLEY, *a worn little woman, comes in, right, with a*

165

duster. She wears a shawl. She goes forward and begins dust-ing PARNELL'S *face.*)

PARNELL

(*As she is about to move on*)

Come back here, my good woman, and put my beard straight.

MRS. GALGOOGLEY

(*Motherly*)

Sure, you're that touchy about your beard, Parnell. (*As she rewipes his beard*) Sure, God help ye, little d'ye know nobody wears them nowadays at all, except an odd mad fellow here and there. Will that do?

PARNELL

Thank you, my good woman, thank you. (*She moves on to* EMMET, *wipes his face and regards him sadly.*)

MRS. GALGOOGLEY

You're frettin', Robert, aren't ye? (*He takes no notice. He is sullen and morose*) Sure God help ye, and you only a child, standin' there forever. (*She passes on to* TONE, *whom she regards severely.* TONE *grins provocatively.*)

MRS. GALGOOGLEY

Well, Cock o' the mornin'.

TONE

How are ye, Brigid Anne? *Bon jour, madame.*

MRS. GALGOOGLEY

Well, aren't you the divil, with that grin of yours and that French lingo. Could you not be sayin' an odd word or two to Robert?

166

TONE

What's the use, Brigid Anne! He goes on regretting he never got living in a free Ireland with old John Philpot's daughter. *Vraiment! La mort vient a tout le mond!*

MRS. GALGOOGLEY

Sure, God help him, he's like my Oweneen the way he frets and fidgets. (*She moves on to the empty slab, and looks at it*) Dan himself will be back from the repairin' men next week. Two of his toes, the American tourists stole off him, and his wee finger and all the curls on the one side of his head.

TONE

The new barbarians . . .

MRS. GALGOOGLEY

Faith, no man is a barbarian nowadays that has money in his arse pocket—savin' your presence. (*As she reaches* LORD EDWARD FITZGERALD) Good mornin', Lord Edward.

LORD EDWARD
(*As she dusts him*)

Morning, Mrs. Galgoogley. Careful with the wound in my neck.

MRS. GALGOOGLEY
(*Dusting carefully*)

I will so. Faith, it was the woeful wound too. (*She moves on to* MITCHELL *whom she dusts respectfully.*)

MITCHELL

Blessin's on you, ma'am. I always did like a little freshen-up in the morning.

167

MRS. GALGOOGLEY

Thank ye, sir. I heard a man sayin' yesterday in Jer O'Brien's pub that the *Jail Journal* was the odesee of the Irish race, whatever that means. Does that please you?

MITCHELL

Faith, it pleases me well.

MRS. GALGOOGLEY

But the other man he was talkin' to rared up, and says he, "How could a great Irishman fight agin the slaves in America and still be more than a spit in the mouth?" And there they went into it like two oul' cats, breakin' faces and glasses and ever'thin'.

MITCHELL

Let them fight away, ma'am. 'Tis only when they can talk without angerin' one another that Ireland will be lost.

MRS. GALGOOGLEY
(*Wandering across*)

'Tis maybe so. . . . (*She goes off, right. The morning begins to brighten. The statues yawn.*)

TONE
(*Fidgeting*)

Les morts—ce sont de tristes personnages! Que leur blême immobilité contraste avec la souple élégance des vivants! (*He bursts into hilarious song.*)

"There's wine from the royal Pope,
And Spanish ale shall give thee hope,
Shall give thee heart and life and hope,
My Dark Rosaleen."

COGGERERS

MITCHELL

Quiet, Tone, for mercy's sake. That puzzling old fool in there will hear you.

LORD EDWARD

Do you, gentlemen, feel anything strange in the air this morning?

PARNELL

In what way strange, my lord?

LORD EDWARD

A sort of restlessness. Everything seems fidgeting.

EMMET

(Lifting head, excitedly)

That's it! I have been trying to analyze it, listening to this fool here raving in French.

TONE

And what's wrong with the French will you tell me?

EMMET

Are you pretending you don't know they are now fighting with the British in Flanders?

TONE

If they are, they have degenerated since Napoleon died.

EMMET

Like our own slaves out there.

PARNELL

(Soothingly)

Enough! Enough! I pray you.

COGGERERS

LORD EDWARD

There *is* something in the air. I *smell* it. (*All the statues start sniffing strongly*) Gunpowder!

EMMET

That's it! That's the way my rockets used to smell in Thomas Street.

TONE
(*Excitedly*)

Vive la Republique!

MITCHELL

Hush, hush! Let us discuss this matter dispassionately. What is your opinion, Parnell?

PARNELL
(*Sniffing*)

Gunpowder my grannie! It's the Liffey. (*All laugh except* EMMET.)

TONE

The Liffey we have always with us. . . . Hush! Here's old Socrates coming. Stupid old classical bookworm! I hate a man who can neither fight nor sing.

ALL

Ssh! (EAMONN O'CURRY *re-enters, back. A heavy overcoat conceals his person. He is ill at ease, and shows suppressed excitement. He looks about him nervously.*)

O'CURRY

Are you there, Mrs. Galgoogley? (*No answer. He breathes more freely. He takes out his watch and consults it. The statues watch him furtively.*)

170

O'CURRY

(*Excitedly*)

Eight-thirty . . . eight-forty-five . . . nine. (*Suddenly, flinging open his overcoat and showing a Volunteer uniform underneath, complete with bandolier and holsters*) The hour is nine, gentlemen!

TONE

(*Involuntarily*)

Mon Dieu! (O'CURRY *swings round in a startled manner, closing the overcoat.*)

O'CURRY

(*Fiercely*)

Is there anyone there? . . . (*Silence*) Good God, I thought I heard a voice . . . as if the dead spoke . . . the dead that died for Ireland. (*To* EMMET, *fiercely*) You poor pale piece of marble, didn't you say that if the flag flew over Dublin Castle for a week, Ireland would be saved? (*The statues do not move*) We'll keep it flying, Emmet. We'll stick it to the mast with our blood. (*Noises off, of pails falling. He swings round, his hands at the holsters.*) By God, I'll not be taken. I'll fight for it like Lord Edward. Who's there? (*The statues look excitedly at each other behind his back, and then resume their poise.* MRS. GALGOOGLEY *re-enters, right, with pails and mops. He is relieved. He breathes freely and speaks.*)

O'CURRY

It's only you, Mrs. Galgoogley.

MRS. GALGOOGLEY

Sure, did I frighten you, Mr. O'Curry? Sure I'm like an oul' scarecrow anyway.

COGGERERS

O'CURRY

It's nothing, ma'am—nothing at all. (*Pause*) The library will be closed all day of course—Easter Monday. I just came in to get a few papers. When you finish, lock up and leave the keys at the gate house.

MRS. GALGOOGLEY

I will so. And I hope you'll have a nice holiday. To the country you'll be goin', I'll bet, sir, with Mrs. O'Curry and the children. Och, sure it'll be the life o' the poor craythurs.

O'CURRY

Well, I don't know that I can manage today. I have a bit o' work to do. It will have to be some other day.

MRS. GALGOOGLEY

Sure, won't the work be after ye, sir, and it still not done anyway. 'Tis little ye get, liftin' the hand for others. Look now at them poor craythurs there that gave love and life and all, and sure, God help them, standin' there. . . . Who gives them a look or a word?

O'CURRY

The look or the word is a small matter, ma'am. They belong to the soul—to the thing that is eternal.

MRS. GALGOOGLEY

'Tis maybe so, but they need dustin' every mornin' all the same. (*She goes to her knees morosely.*)

O'CURRY

How did Dublin look and you comin' along this morning?

172

COGGERERS

MRS. GALGOOGLEY

Look? Sure, jist as it always looks—like a woman paradin'
in all her finery, but a dirty house at home. That's Dublin.

O'CURRY

You didn't notice anythin' unusual?

MRS. GALGOOGLEY

What would there be unusual? The oul' cabbies blowin'
their hands on the quays, and the oceans o' bicycles takin' the
breath out o' ye, and Guinness's porter barrels floatin' down
the Liffey. (*He goes off, in a brown study, back.* MRS. GAL-
GOOGLEY *looks after him.*)

MRS. GALGOOGLEY

Och, sure God help him, sure I think 'tis his stomach that
bees worryin' him. (*She takes the pail and goes off, right. The
statues all become alive instantly and look eagerly at each
other.*)

EMMET
(*Tensely*)
Did you hear? I feel the crash coming. It's here! It's upon
us!

PARNELL

This—is madness, gentlemen! (TONE, EMMET *and* LORD ED-
WARD *laugh sarcastically.*)

EMMET

Same old tune, Parnell. Same old platform stuff.

MITCHELL

Quiet! Quiet! Let us discuss the matter dispassionately. If a
people arrive at the decision that their objective cannot be won
by pacific methods they are justified in resorting to—ssh!

(MRS. GALGOOGLEY *re-enters with pail of water, and interrupts* MITCHELL. *Statues resume their poise.* MRS. GALGOOGLEY *starts washing the floor.* O'CURRY *re-enters.*)

O'CURRY

Finish up and get home quickly, Mrs. Galgoogley.

MRS. GALGOOGLEY

Home? How so, sir?

O'CURRY

It's—it's going to be thunder and lightning. (*Statues rapidly regard each other and then resume their poise.*)

MRS. GALGOOGLEY

Eh? God save us, I dread the thunderin'. Will it be yon forked lightnin' with the tail on it?

O'CURRY

It'll be every sort of lightnin' you ever heard of. Hurry up now. (*Statues again regard each other and resume.*)

MRS. GALGOOGLEY

I will so. It's God that's angry with the people. And Oweneen'll be under the bed. The same divil would rather face a regiment o' soldiers than look at a flash o' lightnin'.

O'CURRY

Is your son not with you this morning?

MRS. GALGOOGLEY

Sure, I knew the furnace wouldn't be gettin' lit so I let him lie on. He didn't get in last night till early this mornin'.

O'CURRY

What was he playin' at, and he just a young fellow yet, keeping such hours?

MRS. GALGOOGLEY

Sure, it's a new invention he and Jerry Turley is workin' on, in Con Carey's cellar. Sure, it bees all hours when he gets in.

O'CURRY

What sort of an invention?

MRS. GALGOOGLEY

Och, sure, the little he tells me . . . somethin' he says, to make the sparkin' plugs of a motor-car spark better.

O'CURRY

I see. . . . Did he say if he was goin' out this morning?

MRS. GALGOOGLEY

He did then. He told me to leave his breakfast in the oven, and I comin' out; that he had to be up at me heels to do a wee bit o' business in the center o' the town. But sure, if it's thunderin', divil the stir he'll stir. Och, sure, what's he but a child?

O'CURRY

Oweneen is a man, Mrs. Galgoogley, and a man must prove himself.

MRS. GALGOOGLEY

Well, sure, so long as he doesn't disgrace me, sir. . . .

O'CURRY

He'll not do that. (*As he crosses*) Good-bye, Mrs. Galgoogley.

MRS. GALGOOGLEY

Good-bye? Sure you'd think, sir, you were goin' to the ends o' the earth instead of Rathmines.

O'CURRY

Well . . . so long, then.

MRS. GALGOOGLEY

Till the mornin', sir. And tell Mrs. O'Curry I be prayin' for her since her operation.

O'CURRY

I will, and thank you. (O'CURRY *goes off, right, putting on his hat as he goes.*)

EMMET

(*Quickly to* MRS. GALGOOGLEY)

Go after him, Mrs. Galgoogley, and wave to him.

MRS. GALGOOGLEY

How so, puttin' bad in me head, Robert Emmet?

EMMET

Because you'll never see him again.

MRS. GALGOOGLEY

(*Starting up*)

What are ye sayin' to me?

PARNELL

Leave her alone, Emmet.

MITCHELL

Don't distress yourself, good woman.

176

COGGERERS

MRS. GALGOOGLEY

Yous are coggerin' there between yous, as if somethin' was there and I not to be seein' it. What are yous at?

EMMET

My words were hasty. Forgive me.

MRS. GALGOOGLEY

I will then, and sure it's not the first time. You're like my Oweneen, Robert Emmet—a hasty little spitfire, and yet a child in ways.

TONE

Och, you'll be crying in a minute, Brigid Anne. *Tant pis! On ne vit que pour mourir.*

MRS. GALGOOGLEY

Och, you! You imp! Divil the word I can have with Robert, without you puttin' in your spake.

TONE

Come on, and give us one of your old come-all-yes.

MRS. GALGOOGLEY

I will not so. And I with not a pick in me stomach but a drop o' tay and the outside cut of a loaf.

LORD EDWARD

But you promised us yesterday morning, Mrs. Galgoogley, and of course as a lady of noble birth, and as a Galgoogley . . .

MRS. GALGOOGLEY

That's right. A Galgoogley . . . If I made a promise, Lord Edward, I'll keep it.

177

TONE

That's the spirit. Wait and I'll give you your doh.

MRS. GALGOOGLEY

I can get me own doh, thank you, Wolfe Tone, with your outrageous and Godforsaken French manners.

EMMET

This is unseemly. I dislike it. I protest.

MRS. GALGOOGLEY

(*Looking at* EMMET)

Och, he frets, like Oweneen.

MITCHELL

You are just morbid and dull, Emmet. There is nothing unseemly in song. We are not a crowd of dull Teutons. We are a people of song and beauty. We are the saviours of idealism in the Nordic jungle. Sing away, Mrs. Galgoogley.

MRS. GALGOOGLEY

I'll sing if Parnell lets me. I knew him the best. One day, as a little girl, Parnell, I touched the tail of your coat in College Green.

PARNELL

Thank you for that, ma'am. Sing by all means, and never—never let us become too respectable.

TONE

Hear! Hear! Give us that one of yours about Dublin.

COGGERERS

(Standing arms akimbo, in loud come-all-ye tones)

"Oh, Dublin is a frowsy dame,
'Tis her's the brazen Tartar,
Her petticoats are Saxon lace,
Her perfume's Guinness's porter.
To see her kneelin' at the Mass
You'd swear she was a martyr
Till Parnell in O'Connell Street
Stares cock-eyed down at her garter."

LORD EDWARD

Excellent!

PARNELL

Very commendable!

MITCHELL

First rate!

TONE

Splendid. I wish I had hands to clap you, Brigid Anne.
Come on, another verse and we'll join in.

MRS. GALGOOGLEY

Well, aren't yous the divils for fun! And amn't I the oul'
fool! (*She starts singing again. All join in except* EMMET,
whose head is drooped very low.)

"She'll sit on Dan O'Connell's steps,
And froth at Anna Liffey
She'll coort a bit with Dick Muldoon
And cod little Father Fiffey.

"Oh, Jerry Mooney is her boy
And Father Matt's her other
And damn the knowing either knows
Such caperin' in a mother.
She'll take a sup with Jer O'Brien
And say an Av' with Father Fiffey.
Fill up with spleen in College Green
And empty all in the Liffey."

(*When the singing stops, all the statues, except* EMMET, *laugh happily.* MRS. GALGOOGLEY *regards* EMMET *in a motherly way.*)

MRS. GALGOOGLEY

You're vexed with me, Robert, and so well ye might be, makin' an oul' fool o' meself and me oul' enough to know better twice over.

TONE

Och, isn't your heart alive, Brigid Anne. Never mind him.

EMMET

It's unseemly and undignified in an hour like this.

ALL

Ssh!

MRS. GALGOOGLEY

In an hour like what?

MITCHELL

Nothing, nothing, Mrs. Galgoogley.

PARNELL

Now, don't distress yourself, good woman.

180

LORD EDWARD

Your life and fate should have taught you discretion, Emmet.

EMMET

I'll say what I'll say, for woe or weal.

MRS. GALGOOGLEY

Sure, it's just that you're short in the temper, Robert, like Oweneen. Many's the drubbin' Oweneen gives me, and then he washes the cup and things for me to make up to me.

EMMET

There you are singing and brawling, and where is Oweneen?

MRS. GALGOOGLEY

Sure, where is he but in bed, and the divil wouldn't waken him, he's that tired.

EMMET

His bed is empty.

LORD EDWARD

Emmet!

TONE

That's not fair!

MITCHELL

Now what's the good in alarming the poor creature? (*She looks at them all uneasily, one after the other. Fear grips her heart.*)

MRS. GALGOOGLEY

Yous are coggerin' there, and yous have somethin' between yous. (*She watches them with fear*) Yous think me an oul' hag without feelin' because I can sing an oul' song. But would I not tear out me eyes and give them to Oweneen to see with? Would I not give me heart's blood to Oweneen to live with? (*Pause. The statues all are very quiet. She stares at them in terror*) What's wrong with Oweneen? Tell me! Tell me, or be Jaysus I'll tear yous down to pieces and flitter yous and thramp on yous. (*Her hands are over her head hysterically. Sobs break from her. She turns away with resolve*) I must go home quick. I must get to Oweneen. 'Tis maybe that a thievin' cut-throat would turn the handle and he'd be murdered and slew in his sleep. (*Suddenly there comes the rapid clattering of rifle fire in the distance, and the sharp reports of revolver shots. These continue at intervals through the play at the places indicated.*)

MRS. GALGOOGLEY

What was that? Mother of Mercy, what was it? Tell me!

LORD EDWARD

Be a brave woman, Mrs. Galgoogley. Be a Galgoogley.

MRS. GALGOOGLEY
(*Appeal*)
I'll be only a woman. . . . Tell me, Lord Edward.

LORD EDWARD

It's what was bound to come, ma'am—guns and the tramp of men again.

MRS. GALGOOGLEY

Merciful God! Oweneen will be killed in his bed.

EMMET

Oweneen is not in his bed. Oweneen is a man. (*Rifle and revolver fire.*)

182

COGGERERS

MRS. GALGOOGLEY

Not in his bed? Have pity on me, Robert. Don't be too hard on me. I'm an oul' woman, wore away with the washin' of floors. Tell me where Oweneen is. (*Revolver and rifle fire.*)

EMMET

Courage, woman. Oweneen's behind the barricades in Stephen's Green.

MRS. GALGOOGLEY
(*In terror*)

The—the barricades? In the Green? . . . He's not! He's not. . . . You're my enemy, Robert Emmett, my enemy and Oweneen's enemy. Oweneen's not grew up, he's only a child. Oh, John Mitchell, John Mitchell, you that saw hearts break! You that saw lives wither away. . . . (*She goes to him in tears.*)

MITCHELL
(*Moved*)

My poor woman, what can I say to you? God, have I not seen enough of this? Must I go on seeing it till the last day ends? (*He bows his head.*)

MRS. GALGOOGLEY
(*Sobbing*)

Parnell! I touched your coat in College Green. I was a little girl with my father. He said, "Touch him, Brigid Anne, he is holy."

PARNELL

I have no words. I have cast them all to the winds. . . . (*Sudden rapid volley of shots*) That, that you hear, is the words of the new generation, and I am too old to read them.

183

COGGERERS

MRS. GALGOOGLEY

(Wringing her hands)

Yous knew this was comin' and yous wouldn't tell me! Yous villains and cut-throats and stinkin' coggerers! I that always had the wee word for yous and the wipe of me duster, when the patent leather people passed yous and the high men with big books. And did I not sing for yous the song of the greedy oul' bitch that yous all died for. *(Volley of shots)* I know what it is that's up with yous! Yous are jealous of Oweneen and the way his strong arms can fling a hundred o' coal on his shoulder—jealous of the pant of his breath, the cry of his blood and the ring of his heart beats. *(Shots)* Yous coggered together to get him into that corner there *(She pointed to the vacant corner)*, to be one of yourselves, yous wicked, jealous, dead oul' vagabonds! But yous'll not get him. My Oweneen has warm blood that he will give not to yous, nor to that oul' bitch that wanders O'Connell Street *(Volley of shots)*, but to some little soft bit of a girl who will give him back in exchange the livin' life; do yous hear, the livin' life! I'll go out to my Oweneen now, and I will put my woman's body round his, as it was long ago in the beginning. My seven curses on yous and my seven curses on the oul' bitch yous died the death for! *(A volley. She staggers across the floor towards the door, wrapping her old shawl about her. The statues look at each other. Rifle and revolver fire.)*

MITCHELL

(Murmuring)

Poor woman . . . poor woman . . . *(As she nears the door, it is flung back and* OWENEEN, *a boy of about nineteen, staggers in, wounded. He is dressed partly in uniform and wears a bandolier. Blood has stained his tunic. His rifle falls*

184

from his hands. He is pale and grimy with powder. The statues lean forward and look excitedly.)

OWENEEN
(*Staggering*)

Mother! . . .

MRS. GALGOOGLEY
(*Staring at him*)

Oweneen! Mother o' God! . . . (*She runs forward and catches him, preventing him from falling*) What foolery is this you're at now? (*She sees the blood on his breast*) Am I not always—God! Blood! . . . Oweneen's blood. . . . Yous have got him, yous villains and vipers! . . . Me one little bit of riches that I was hidin' from yous. Yous found him out; yous ferreted him out. . . .

OWENEEN
(*Weakly*)

Listen to me, mother. . . .

MRS. GALGOOGLEY
(*Sadly*)

Aye then, son. Put your mouth into me ear and whisper it anont to them.

OWENEEN

I want to lie down, mother. . . . Put me on the floor. (*She gently lowers his body to the floor. She puts her shawl under his head and kneeling by his side, leans over him. Rifle and revolver fire*) Mother, I—I'm afraid. . . .

MRS. GALGOOGLEY

Of what, son? Sure they'll not find you here, unless them villains there tell.

185

OWENEEN

'Tis not of them I'm afraid, mother. It's of the pain in me breast. (*With weak passion*) I—I don't want to die. . . . I want to live. . . . I—I—I want to be twinty-one one day and to—to have a party and singin' . . . (*His head falls back.*)

MRS. GALGOOGLEY

(Almost insanely, as if talking to herself)

They've kilt him on me, the villains and vipers! Me one little dropeen o' gold, me one little sprig with the green leaves on it. (*She is peering closely into his face, the woman in her fighting for hope.*)

OWENEEN

(Painfully)

It was all cruel and awful. . . . I didn't know anythin' could be so terrible. . . . (*A volley of shots*) I wanted to shut me eyes and call on God. . . . Then the pain came and I could taste the blood in me mouth . . . and I crawled down the lane. . . . I knew you'd be here. . . . Mother, I want to live. . . . I want to sit and think all over again about everythin'. . . . Will I be all right, mother? Tell me! Is it just the cold of the ground that's got into me bones? (*Volley of shots.*)

MRS. GALGOOGLEY

Just that, son, with God's help. Sure if there's a God at all. . . .

OWENEEN

What has God to do with it, Mother, when the guns start roarin'? (*Shots*) I'm shiverin' and it's gettin' dark. . . . I wish I could have gone on till I stopped growin'. . . . I'm an inch and a half short of what me da was, and you said I'd be taller nor he was. . . . Twinty-one, we said, didn't we? (*He turns his head gently and dies.* MRS. GALGOOGLEY *looks*

186

down at him tearfully, but calmly. She crosses herself slowly.
A moment passes. Shots. She lifts her head fatalistically and
looks round at the statues.)

MRS. GALGOOGLEY

(*Slowly*)

Yous villains and vagabones, yous have taken him from me, with your plottin' and coggerin'.

MITCHELL

You poor lonely creature, my heart bleeds for you.

MRS. GALGOOGLEY

There's no blood in your heart, John Mitchell, to bleed for anyone, so let ye hould your whisht. The oul' whore ye died for drank it all. (*Volley of shots.*)

EMMET

Slut! I'm ashamed of you! What kind of talk is that for the mother of a hero? You should lift up your heart and be proud.

MRS. GALGOOGLEY

Did Sarah Curran lift up her heart and be proud, Robert Emmet, when the dogs licked your blood in Green Street?

EMMET

(*Tensely*)

She did! She did!

MRS. GALGOOGLEY

So *you* think. But she only cried herself sick because her lover was dead.

EMMET

That's a wicked calumny. You ought to be ashamed of yourself. Slut and harridan!

187

COGGERERS

LORD EDWARD

That'll do, Emmet! Can't you see she's distraught.

PARNELL

The poor woman is right. This dying with honor with a bullet in your guts is a relic of savagery. It's time it was buried at the crossroads of the nations. So long as there is a hope of constitutional—

LORD EDWARD, EMMET, WOLFE TONE
(Together)

Bah! (PARNELL *lapses into silence. A silence follows.* MRS. GALGOOGLEY *regards them all sadly and then looks down at* OWENEEN.)

MRS. GALGOOGLEY
(Resigned)

Ah, sure, God help yous all standin' there forever and ever and no man at all takin' the least notice of yous, and God help me too standin' here with my little dead maneen. (*Rapid rifle fire.*)

TONE

Sure if you could only see it, Brigid Anne, your maneen was more than ten Samsons that stayed at home.

LORD EDWARD

We're all proud of him, Mrs. Galgoogley. Aren't you, Emmet?

EMMET

I take off my hat in spirit to the dead who die for Ireland.

MRS. GALGOOGLEY
(Softly)

Do you mean to Oweneen, Robert?

EMMET

I do. The people will remember him. Put him up here among us. This is his place.

MRS. GALGOOGLEY
(*With pathetic eagerness*)

Do yous want him? Honest now, and do yous? Sure he hasn't a clean shirt or nothin' on him?

ALL

Put him amongst us. He is ours now. We claim him.

MRS. GALGOOGLEY

Aye then . . . he's yours. . . . I'll put him there in the vacant place where Dan O'Connell was before the Americans took lumps off him with their penknives. (*She draws* OWENEEN's *body tenderly towards the low marble slab, and places it upon it. The statues look round at the body as she steps back from him.*)

PARNELL
(*Gravely*)

Gentlemen, we have added to our company an illustrious patriot. I call upon Mr. Emmet to say a few fitting words to mark this occasion.

EMMET
(*Oratorically*)

Gentlemen, no tears for the dead who die for Ireland. Let us rejoice that blood is still rebellious in Irish veins and that the end was not with you or me or any of us—that the end will not be until all our manacles are riven. In spirit I salute this, my brother, who is come to his rightful home.

189

COGGERERS

TONE
(Softly)
Le roi est mort. Vive le roi. . . . *(Volley of shots.*)

ALL
Amen. We salute our brother.

MRS. GALGOOGLEY
(Softly weeping)
There now, yous wanted him, and yous have him now. Sure who am I to be grumblin', and I wore with the washin' of floors. Sure 'tis maybe that I'll be cryin' needlessly on the Liffey quays where the men do be talkin' and spittin', or on O'Connell Bridge with the world and his wife passin'; and forgettin', when I'll be havin' a sup in Jer O'Brien's, that God and the dead know best. Let yous be good now to Oweneen, and I away, and let yous not have him frettin' after me. *(She looks down at him and smiles, then turns slowly and goes out meanderingly.)*

PARNELL
There is Life going out there—poor, ragged, thwarted, buffetted, beaten and yet living, and with hope in the heart.

EMMET
And there is the music of Liberty! Listen! *(From without come the rapid reports of rifles and revolvers and the spitting of Thompson guns)* The symphony of Freedom, gentlemen! What notes on a thundering scale! What grand crescendos! And what immortal musicians!

The Curtain Falls Slowly